WOMEN IN MEDICINE — 1976

RECENT MACY FOUNDATION PUBLICATIONS

The University and Medicine: The Past, the Present, and Tomorrow, edited by John Z. Bowers and Elizabeth F. Purcell

Minorities in Medicine: From Receptive Passivity to Positive Action 1966–76, by Charles E. Odegaard

Campus Health Programs, edited by Willard Dalrymple and Elizabeth F. Purcell

Recent Trends in Medical Education, edited by Elizabeth F. Purcell

Advances in American Medicine: Essays at the Bicentennial, edited by John Z. Bowers and Elizabeth F. Purcell

A Half-Century of American Medical Education: 1920–1970, by Vernon W. Lippard

Teaching the Basic Medical Sciences: Human Biology, edited by John Z. Bowers and Elizabeth F. Purcell

The University Medical Center and the Metropolis, edited by Eli Ginzberg and Alice M. Yohalem

Schools of Public Health: Present and Future, edited by John Z. Bowers and Elizabeth F. Purcell

*   *   *   *

A complete catalogue of books in print
will be sent upon request

Edited by
Carolyn Spieler

WOMEN IN MEDICINE – 1976

Report of a Macy Conference

Josiah Macy, Jr. Foundation
One Rockefeller Plaza, New York, New York 10020

© 1977 Josiah Macy, Jr. Foundation
All rights reserved
Library of Congress Catalog Number: 77-82299
ISBN: 0-914362-21-6
Manufactured by Waverly Press, Baltimore, Maryland
Distributed by the Independent Publishers Group
14 Vanderventer Avenue, Port Washington, New York 11050

Contents

v

Contents

Foreword

The most striking improvement in the constitution of the body of American medical students is the sharp increase in the number of women. It is a phenomenon of the past decade and results from a variety of initiatives by philanthropic and federal sources stimulated by the Women's Liberation Movement. Yet, given the momentum of the liberation movement, one may wonder why the influx of female medical students has not been even greater.

The efforts of the Josiah Macy, Jr. Foundation to increase the admission of women students to medical schools began in 1966. Our primary goal was to draw national attention to the disparity between the number of women in medicine in the United States and in other countries of the Western World. These modest efforts soon became coterminous with those of other organizations and with the Women's Liberation Movement, and there was little, if any, need for philanthropic foundations to continue to invest in the field.

The strong influence of the rising tide of female medical students soon became apparent, and in 1975 the directors of the Macy Foundation agreed we should conduct a study to explore and evaluate this impact. Elizabeth McAnarney, M.D., assistant professor of pediatrics, psychiatry, and medicine at the University of Rochester School of Medicine and Dentistry, directed the

vii

study: her inquiry took her to eleven academic medical centers and the Radcliffe Institute for Independent Studies, and included a thorough search of the literature and the development of a data bank. We hope that her report, which is published in this volume, will convey to the reader at least some of the clarity of her work.

Mary I. Bunting, Ph.D., president-emeritus of Radcliffe College, and our first collaborator in assisting women in medicine, agreed to serve as chairman of the Macy conference for which Dr. McAnarney's study served as the background document. The conference, also reported in this volume, was held in Aspen, Colorado, 7–10 September 1976.

As we enter the most interesting phase of the new era of women in American medicine, some of the questions we are asking include: What will be their career choices? What will be their impact on the structure of residency training? And reluctantly, but necessarily: What will be the percentage of "part-time" and "full-time" doctors? Women are making new and major demands for a radical restructuring of medical education — some of which are shocking to entrenched department chairman. It appears that there will of necessity be some bending on both sides. But these are some of the questions we should ask Elizabeth McAnarney and Mary Bunting to answer for us five to ten years from now.

John Z. Bowers, M.D.
President
Josiah Macy, Jr. Foundation

May 1977

Afterthoughts by Way of Introduction

❦

Mary I. Bunting

It has been my privilege to chair both the 1966 Macy conference on Women *for* Medicine and the 1976 conference on Women *in* Medicine, from which the material in this report has been drawn. The shift in prepositions is significant. In 1966 our primary interest was in increasing the number of women entering medicine in the United States; by 1976 they were well represented in our medical schools and our concerns had shifted to the quality of their experiences, the opportunities open to them, and their effectiveness as physicians and as individuals.

Although all of the medical schools in the country had opened to women by 1966, more than 90 percent of the applicants were men. Among developed nations, only in Japan was the fraction of licensed women physicians smaller than the 9.1 percent practicing in the United States. In the intervening ten years a marked increase in the demand for access to quality medical care has brought many changes, including Medicare and Medicaid legislation, the debate about national health insurance, and a rise in the interest of young people in pursuing medical careers.

In the last five years, particularly, there has been a dramatic increase in the number of women applying to and admitted by our medical schools. In 1966 they constituted 9 percent of the first-year class; by 1976 they made up almost 24 percent of all first-year medical students, and at least one-third of the class in several of the most prestigious schools. The expansion in relative as well as absolute numbers was all the more remarkable because it took place in face of keen competition from men. No comparable shift has occurred at the graduate level in arts

1

and sciences, where total enrollments have leveled off; a similar rise in popularity and in the proportion of women admitted has, however, been noted in law schools and, very recently, in schools of business administration and engineering. Evidently women interested in professional careers are not following lines of least resistance in the 1970s.

Participants in the 1976 conference were eager to assess the experiences of medical women at this time. How are things going for the new generation of students, and how are they doing? What if any impact has the increase in their numbers had on medical school procedures; on faculty and staff attitudes and expectations; on relations between male and female students? How free are women to enter the specialties that interest them most, and which do they choose? What impact are they having at the graduate level, and how are they coping with the demands of residency training? What decisions are they making about marriage; about having children? How many years do they practice? What still needs to be done to maximize the lifetime contributions of medical women? What if any effect will the growing number of women physicians have on the availability, quality, and cost of health care? What other outcomes are anticipated? Who is monitoring the changes that are taking place? A large number of these questions was touched on during the course of the conference.

Recent Trends

To undergird future research, but also to alert all units of our medical institutions, every department should be urged to keep accurate records, broken down by sex of student, attendance, and progress, as well as of staff responsibilities, plans, and promotions. Detailed comparative studies could provide valuable clues; investigators in departments of psychology, sociology, anthropology, business administration, and related fields are urged to take note while sociodegradable data are still available. Which factors accelerate and which retard the elimination of stereotypic thinking and categorical decisions? Clear institutional objectives and sound relevant data would go a long way toward eliminating prejudices and improving procedures and programs.

It is important to realize that the encouraging improvements in attitudes toward women students are not necessarily a consequence of an increase in their numbers, particularly at a time when competition for places in medical schools, and, later for desirable residencies, is unusually keen. Examples of heightened tensions associated with expanding enrollments and competition come readily to mind. All too often in academia, for example, it has been in those disciplines with the strongest women undergraduates that faculty have been slowest to promote women to positions of tenure.

Apparently the social forces responsible for more open admission of women to medical schools have also brought greater sensitivity to their needs. Once initiated, fair treatment carries its own momentum, especially when it is visibly favored by top management. Even male chauvinists enjoy winning approval from superiors. The appointment of able women to prestigious committees can have a positive influence on receptive men, setting off chain reactions of sensitization that affect behavior throughout an institution. The old adage still holds in medicine, however: "the higher, the fewer." Judgments concerning future promise are necessarily subjective. If women are not expected to make truly significant advances, it is difficult to detect, let alone nourish, the originality, talent, and courage that some possess. Letters of recommendation that describe a woman's past accomplishments glowingly, but fail to mention her potentiality for future growth, should always be suspect.

Given the prejudices directed toward scientifically inclined young women — against their curiosity, persistence, stubborness, casual dress, and, sometimes, their inarticulation — that persist in homes, schools, and colleges, pickings are slimmer than they should be at the professorial levels in medicine and other disciplines requiring rigorous scientific preparation. Thus it is all the more important that those women who have the ability and training become visible. Until we have appreciable numbers of highly qualified women physicians in academic posts, the environment will be deficient for men as well as for women, for faculty as well as for students, and we shall not know what their full potentials might be.

As the barriers are lowered and it becomes more acceptable for women to enter medicine, a greater diversity of women can be expected to apply for enrollment. Until recently, toughness of character has been the first prerequisite, which limited the pool of talent, just as the demands of modern political campaigning limit the kinds of people who are willing to run for public office. With greater diversity among the applicants, medical school committees will have a wider range of choices and far greater opportunity to find out which traits and which early experiences offer the best preparation for women entering medicine and for their later productivity and career satisfactions.

Remaining Problems

Members of both sexes are frequently confused about roles. Both are more accustomed to thinking of females as helpmates or assistants than as intellectual or organizational leaders. Women who do brilliantly in school are not necessarily expected to advance the frontiers later. Even more troublesome to women physicians are cultural concepts about a woman's role in bringing up her children. It may be that, as women gain more control over the planning of their own families, they feel greater responsibility for the conditions under which their children are raised. In any event, our culture holds this role to be of key importance and provides few attractive alternatives.

The suggestion that accredited homemaker groups be organized to provide trained care for children and/or the elderly was greeted enthusiastically. It would be ideal if one could join such a group on a prepaid basis, with a choice of a regular assistant and an understanding about substitutes. Certainly the need for a variety of experimental approaches to the problem and for careful evaluation of results is evident. One hopes that community groups and qualified research units will join forces to provide better services and better answers than we now have. Funds should be made available by the Department of Health, Education, and Welfare and other sources to support promising pilot projects in this area. In the absence of valid data, problems tend to reinforce old stereotypes and engender feelings of doubt or scorn, depending on the degree of one's involvement. Research as well as rhetoric is needed to build a just society.

Turning to the problems that women face because of the nature of medical training and practice, again one finds a complex mixture of inherent and contrived difficulties. The fact that the physician must deal with sickness and pain, anxiety and death, often under circumstances when speed and accuracy in diagnosis and treatment are critically important, is bound to result in severe pressures on all physicians. In addition, there are pressures caused by the rigors of training and practice, particularly graduate training with its sanctification of the "hundred-hour week." The considerable time that must be spent on routine hospital chores that have negligible educational value, together with the apparent lack of objective criteria for evaluating progress, suggest that education is a by-product rather than the central purpose of "graduate training." These concerns are doubly troublesome to the female resident who knows that the late twenties are her optimum years for childbearing.

Recommendations for Action

With the entrance of more women into graduate training and with the prevailing doubts about its design and effectiveness, it is not surprising that the conferees gave high priority to a reexamination of residency programs. Older physicians who refer patients to our hospitals are frequently out of touch with modern advances in diagnosis and therapy. Perhaps they could share some of the hospital load and participate in some of the learning as a form of continuing education. Their experience could be as valuable to younger physicians as contact with recent developments would be for the older doctors.

The conference strengthened my own belief that the time

has come for thorough, experimental studies of graduate education. Entire hospitals should be reorganized, in some instances, in order to deal with all dimensions of the issue, including the economics of the institution. Essential to the experiments would be the development of criteria for judging the educational progress of house staff—using the word "educational" in the broadest sense. The value of such criteria and methods would extend to practice beyond formal training programs and should be of particular benefit to women, enabling those who are capable and conscientious to establish their qualifications.

The scope and importance of such comprehensive experimental programs call for federal support through long-term grants or contracts. In addition to these major undertakings, funding should also be made available for smaller, related experiments designed to test specific components. In the late 1960s, programs for women physicians to reenter medicine or train for a specialty on flexible residencies were negotiated by the Radcliffe Institute with support from the Macy Foundation: the subsequent careers of these physicians illustrate the value of such pinpointed explorations. The wastefulness for the individual and society of discarding medical school graduates because they cannot meet the obligations of the "hundred-hour week" is readily apparent. There is undoubtedly room for a variety of graduate programs to meet the different but legitimate circumstances and objectives of different physicians. The Radcliffe Institute experiment showed that a little flexibility at a crucial point in a woman physician's life could enable her to complete the training for the goals to which she aspired. She was then ready and did move forward into a responsible full-time post that would otherwise have been beyond her reach.

Another area of particular concern to the conferees, many of whom were drawn from academic medicine, is the small number of women professors in our medical schools. While it is recognized that the impact of the female presence has not yet reached its height, there is little confidence that the system will give women a fair chance when it does. The importance of women helping women to plan ahead, to understand the system, to use it and improve it was emphasized.

One of the minor problems examined is the fear that increased numbers of women in medicine might cause (or is already reflecting) a loss of status for the profession. The same might apply to certain specialties such as family practice. It is the inadequacy of current yardsticks, such as "patients seen per day," when the common complaint is the impersonality of health care, that permits invidious distinctions to be made. The challenge here is to engage in studies that demonstrate the quality of the services rendered. Medicine can be a model educational system for professional women and for minorities. If the problems in this very demanding and very visible field can be solved, the answers, and the fact that there are answers, should serve as a guide and a stimulus to advances in many other disciplines.

The Impact of Medical Women in United States Medical Schools

❧

Elizabeth R. McAnarney

"The reason firm, the temperate will,
Endurance, foresight, strength, and skill;
A perfect woman, nobly planned,
To warn, to comfort, and command."
William Wordsworth
"She Was a Phantom of Delight"

In both the mid-1800s and the mid-1970s significant changes occurred for women in medicine: both eras were marked by an increasing number of women entering the profession and by a gradual lowering of the barriers against them.

The women's movements and societal changes were the background against which developments in the medical center milieu occurred. An Englishwoman, Elizabeth Blackwell, struggled and finally gained entrance to an American medical school; in 1849 she became the first woman to graduate;[1] the first American woman graduate was Lydia Folger Fowler. Other noted women physicians in the 1800s were: Ann Preston, dean of the Female Medical College of Pennsylvania at a time when similar institutions were facing extinction, and Mary Putnam Jacobi, who in 1880 was the first woman to be elected to the New York Academy of Medicine.[2]

During the late 1800s the number of women's medical colleges increased, and females gradually began to gain access to previously all-male institutions. By 1910 there were 13,687 women physicians in this country.[3] The women's medical colleges had difficulties in surviving, however, and in 1910 only two remained.

From the early 1900s to the 1960s women graduates of American medical colleges ranged from 2.6 percent (116) in

9

1910 to a maximum of 12.1 percent (612) in 1949, dropping to 7.3 percent (503) in 1965. In 1944 only 9 percent of the nation's medical schools were enrolling only men; the last school to admit women to an all-male instituion was Jefferson Medical College in Philadelphia in 1960.[4] The last medical school to become coeducational, however, was the Women's Medical College of Philadelphia, which accepted its first male students in 1970!

The major deterrents to the enrollment of more women in medical centers in the first half of the twentieth century were the concerns of admissions personnel that women would not be as productive during a professional lifetime as their male colleagues, and the conflicts many women experienced between a career and marriage. There was also minimal support from society for a woman who entered medicine.

A comparison of the mid–1960s and the mid–1970s shows a marked increment in the number of women enrolled in American medical schools (Table 1, Figure 1). In 1964–65, 7.7 percent of all students enrolled were women; in 1975–76, 20.5 percent were women. This increase came about as the result of several historical occurrences: federal legislation prohibiting discrimination on the basis of sex; private philanthropic sup-

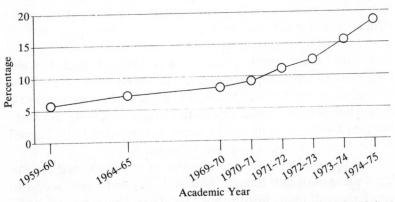

Figure 1. Percentage of Women Enrolled in Medical Schools in the United States (Selected Years, 1959–75).

Source: Adapted from "Medical Education in the United States 1974–1975," *Journal of the American Medical Association 75th Annual Report* 234, no. 13 (29 December 1975): Table 11, 1338. Copyright 1975, American Medical Association.

Table 1. Women in United States Medical Schools
(Selected Years from 1939–75)

Academic Year	Women Applicants[a]		Women in Entering Class		Total Women Enrolled		Women Graduates	
	Number	Percent	Number	Percent	Number	Percent	Number	Percent
1939–40	632	5.4	296[b]	5.0	1,145	5.4	253	5.0
1949–50	1,390	5.7	387	5.5	1,806	7.2	595	10.7
1959–60	1,026	6.9	494	6.0	1,710	5.7	405	5.7
1964–65	1,731	9.0	786	8.9	2,503	7.7	503	6.8
1969–70	2,289	9.4	952	9.2	3,390	9.0	700	8.4
1970–71	2,734	10.9	1,256	11.1	3,894	9.6	827	9.2
1971–72	3,737	12.8	1,693	13.7	4,755	10.9	860	9.0
1972–73	5,480	15.2	2,315	16.9	6,099	12.8	924	8.9
1973–74	7,202	17.8	2,743	19.6	7,731[c]	15.4[c]	1,264	11.1
1974–75	8,712	20.4	3,260	22.3	9,786	18.1	1,706	13.4
1975–76[d]	9,575	22.6	3,647	23.8	11,417	20.5	2,200	16.2

SOURCE: Exclusive of figures for 1939–40 and for 1975–76 women applicants in entering class and enrolled, American Medical Association Group on Medical Education, "Medical Education in the United States 1975–1976," *Journal of the American Medical Association 76th Annual Report* 236, no. 26 (27 December 1976): Table 13, 2962. Copyright 1976, American Medical Association.

[a] From the study of applicants, Association of American Medical Colleges.
[b] E. F. Potthoff, "The Future Supply of Medical Students in the United States, *Journal of Medical Education* 35 (March 1960): Table 1, 224.
[c] Harvard did not provide enrollment figures.
[d] W. F. Dubé, "Datagram: Women Enrollment and Its Minority Component in United States Medical Schools," *Journal of Medical Education* 51 (August 1976): 692.

port of studies of women and medical education; and changes in societal attitudes. A major research question and the focus of this report, therefore, is: "What is the impact of the increasing number of women on the academic medical centers?"

This question is a difficult one. Are observed developments in the academic medical centers a result of the growing number of women students, societal change, or a combination of factors? If women report changes in certain areas, are these true only for the females or are there more general trends that affect students of both sexes? For example, John Romano wrote in his essay, "More Point than Counterpoint," published on the occasion of the fiftieth anniversary of the University of Rochester School of Medicine:

> . . . we also find that for several reasons there appears to be less intimacy between teacher and student as well as more formal structure of student activities through the establishment of student committees. We learn, too, that in their attempts to combat isolation and anonymity students seek and even help to create small student-faculty groups and continue to use the summer and year-out fellowship to pursue their special interests. Many students have been much concerned with the notion of relevance, particularly in the subject matter of the pre-clinical periods, and at times, have become impatient and dissatisfied with their teaching both in method and in substance.[5]

House officers at large medical centers describe their feeling of serving as technicians to patients rather than as their doctors or caretakers. Women and men students, house staff, and faculty express concern about depersonalization in the larger health care settings. This milieu affects all students, house staff, and faculty—not just women.

Attitudinal changes take time. Negative attitudes about women as physicians have evolved over many years in this country. Longshore expressed this sentiment as follows:

> Woman, having so long been regarded and so long regarded herself, alike, intellectually and physically inferior to man, it will require time before she can realize the great fact that her own sex can be rendered equally qualified to assume all the responsibilities of a profession hitherto wholly monopolized by him. . .[6]

It may be too early to document the full impact on the medical centers of the increasing number of women. The major purpose of this study was to clarify what changes have occurred in a sample of American academic medical centers during the last decade, possibly as a result of this influx. The focus of the study was on women physicians and medical students in the academic medical centers; it did not include women in practice.

Between March and June 1976 site visits were made to eleven academic medical centers — approximately 9 percent of the nation's 116 medical schools — and to the Radcliffe Institute for Independent Study: Harvard, Johns Hopkins, Medical College of Pennsylvania, Meharry, Pennsylvania State (Hershey), Stanford, University of California at San Diego and San Francisco, University of Michigan, University of Rochester, and Vanderbilt.

The selection of these institutions was based on the total number of enrolled students; percentage of women entering the first-year class in 1974; geographic location; and institutional status. Private and public centers with both large and

Table 2. Characteristics of Study Institutions

School	Total Student Body (1975–76)	Percent Women in First Year Class (1973–74)	Geographic Region	Public vs. Private
California, San Diego	324	12	Southwest	Public
California, San Francisco	591	28	West	Public
Harvard	700	28	Northeast	Private
Johns Hopkins	510	15	Mid-Atlantic	Private
Medical College of Pennsylvania	365	75	Northeast	Private
Meharry	412	27	South	Private
Michigan	976	25	Midwest	Public
Pennsylvania State	356	75	Northeast	Public and Private
Rochester	402	18	Northeast	Private
Stanford	390	26	West	Private
Vanderbilt	332	11	South	Private

Table 3. Individual Contacts Made in the Course of the Study

	Administrators	Medical Students	Faculty	House Staff
Female	12	108	67	34
Male	23	46	38	21
Total	35	154	105	55

small student bodies, high and low percentages of women, and divergent geographic regions of the country were chosen (Table 2). All of the institutions agreed to the visits.

A variety of individuals was interviewed in each center. The deans' offices arranged meetings with male and female medical students, house staff, faculty, and administrators. Emphasis was placed on seeing males and females in each setting in order to gain an understanding of problems both faced, and to find out the males' perspective of the issues of women in medicine. Informal meetings were also arranged. Table 3 indicates the numbers of individuals contacted. This list includes all individuals interviewed, and the students, house staff, and faculty who completed a pilot questionnaire at the University of Rochester: in all, contact was made with thirty-five administrators; 154 medical students; 105 faculty; and fifty-five house staff.

Standard protocols initially piloted at the University of Rochester were used to ensure uniformity of data gathering (see Appendixes 1 and 2). Most administrators and staff were seen individually; medical students and house staff in groups. Detailed notes were kept, and they were summarized at the end of each day. Because the investigator sought the impressions of individuals interviewed, quantitative data are limited. Additional data were gathered from published reports and from unpublished data shared by investigators.

* * * *

The findings are divided into the following sections: medical students; faculty; and house staff.

Medical Students

Being a woman in the medical profession forces you to deal with many insecurities, many difficult questions, and in my case has allowed me to answer some of these problems with confidence in a new-found ability that has grown as I have matured these four years. . . . It may have been a little more difficult for me than my male counterpart to do well, but overcoming that difficulty perhaps gives me an advantage in the long run. . .

Female fourth-year medical student

Overview

Admissions personnel at the centers visited say that women and men medical students as a group have broader backgrounds and higher academic ratings than did their counterparts a decade ago. In addition, today's students are characterized as challenging, open, well-informed, and interested in the world around them. In 1972, 28.9 percent of the first-year students had an *A* average on entry to medical school; two years later 39.3 percent did.[7] Data from the Medical College Admission Test show an increment in each of the areas, comparing 1955–56 to 1975–76: verbal ability, quantitative thinking, general information, and science, with scores of 524:575,

Table 4. Mean Medical College Admission Test Scores of Accepted Applicants During the Past 21 Years*

Year	Verbal Ability	Quantitative Ability	General Information	Science
1955–56	524	528	527	522
1965–66	541	583	565	549
1975–76	575	620	550	615

SOURCE: American Medical Association Group on Medical Education, "Medical Education in the United States 1975–1976," *Journal of the American Medical Association 76th Annual Report* 236, no. 26 (27 December 1976): Table 17, 2963. Copyright 1976, American Medical Association.

* From the study of applicants, Association of American Medical Colleges.

Table 5. Students Admitted to 110 Medical Schools, 1972–73
Through 1974–75, and Still in School or Graduated, June 1975

| | Men Enrolled/Graduated | | | Women Enrolled/Graduated | | |
Year	Admitted	Number	Percent	Admitted	Number	Percent
1972–73	10,955	10,628	97.0	2,135	2,048	95.9
1973–74	10,962	10,621	96.9	2,591	2,470	95.3
1974–75	11,060	10,925	98.8	3,092	3,047	98.5

SOURCE: "Medical Education in the United States 1974–75," *Journal of the American Medical Association 75th Annual Report* 234, no. 13 (29 December 1975): Table 12, 1338. Copyright 1975, American Medical Association.

528:620, 527:550, and 522:615, respectively (Table 4).[8] Women continue to do better than men in verbal ability and general information, but not as well on quantitative ability and science subtests.

Attrition rates are difficult to interpret unless the destination of the student is clarified. A 1966 study reported almost twice the number of women dropouts as males;[9] more recent data show that, of students admitted in 1972–73, 95.9 percent of the women and 97 percent of the men are either still enrolled or graduated as of June 1975 (Table 5);[10] the 1.1 percent difference is less than previously reported. Most deans in the medical centers visited think that in most cases both men and women drop out for personal reasons, even if the student is officially listed as an academic failure. The majority of admissions personnel report that the overall decrease in attrition for all students reflects improved admissions procedures and the availability of motivated, bright students from whom to choose.

The last decade has been marked by major developments for female medical students in the medical centers. Their presence in greater numbers has affected admissions policies; counseling services; peer interactions; faculty-student communication; and to some extent physical facilities. Few improvements have been effected in the number of female role models, or in the social isolation and frustrations of day-to-day existence felt by some females. In fact new problems for some, such as a rise in the number of divorces and more covert discrimination, are being clarified.

Admissions

Between 1960 and 1975 there was a marked rise in the percentage of women applying and matriculating to the nation's medical schools. The Joint Committee on the Status of Women at Harvard Medical School (HMS), Harvard School of Dental Medicine (HSDM), and Harvard School of Public Health (HSPH) reported:

> The Committee is pleased to note the increase in women applicants accepted for matriculation by HMS, HSDM, and HSPH. At present, women comprise about one-third of the classes of 1978 at both HMS and HSDM. Likewise at the School of Public Health about 37% of the students accepted were women.[11]

In reviewing the admission of women to medical school in the 1960s, some educators thought that the relatively low percentage reflected a dearth of qualified applicants. Others postulated that even though this was partially true, admissions policies and certain interviewers' unwelcoming attitudes deterred some capable females from pursuing medical careers. Data on a national basis show an overall increment from 1,731 women applicants in 1964–65 to 9,575 in 1975–76 (Table 1); the percentage of applicants approximately equalled that of women entering for most years.

Admissions officers are able to document the small number of women applicants to individual medical schools in the 1960s compared to the 1970s. In the experience of what I shall call School A, the number of applicants was approximately four times as great for the class of 1978 (entering in 1974) as it was for the class of 1972 (entering in 1968) (Table 6). At School B, which had been established longer than School A, the number of female applicants was nearly eighteen times higher in 1975 (class of 1979) than in 1959 (class of 1963) (Table 7). All data indicate that the pool of women candidates is greater in the 1970s than it was in the 1960s.

The difficulties some female candidates reported they expe-

Table 6. Admissions Data (School A)

Class of	Total Applications	Female Applications	Percent	Total Class	Females in Class	Percent
1972	1,906	174	9	48	4	8
1974	2,461	282	12	69	8	12
1976	2,521	532	21	82	19	23
1978	2,575	632	25	91	17	19

Table 7. Admissions Data (School B)

Class of	Total Applications	Female Applications	Percent	Total Class	Females in Class	Percent
1963	1,031	61	6	71	5	7
1969	1,160	83	7	70	2	3
1974	1,648	138	8	79	8	10
1979	4,523	1,063	24	97	26	27

rienced when being interviewed for admission bear further consideration. Some of the specific problems noted were: comments that women belong at home and not in medical school; questions about dating, marriage, childbearing, and childrearing discussed exclusively with women and not with men; generalizations about the female role directed at individual women; questions about whether the applicant would use her medical training; and, in general, discourtesy on the part of some interviewers. Not all women applicants prior to the 1970s had such experiences, but the complaints were frequent enough to be considered a problem.

Of fifty-three female students in one school who responded to the survey, thirty-eight had not experienced any such comments in their interviews for admission between 1971 and 1975; fifteen reported some negative remarks in the following forms: "We get less mileage out of our women doctors"; "Women physically may be less able to practice medicine (fatigue, cramps during menstrual periods)"; "Why don't you want to be a nurse?" Most of the women thought these comments reflected an individual interviewer's attitude, however, rather than the policy of the admissions committee or the individual university.

In most medical schools in the 1970s the ungracious attitudes of admissions interviewers have diminished. In fact when first- and fourth-year students compared their individual medical school admissions interviews they reported marked improvement over the three-year period, 1971–74, in the number of questions asked exclusively of women.

A female applicant in the mid-1970s, faced with an intrusive comment or question, would be more likely to tell the interviewer she thought his remark was inappropriate than would her earlier counterpart. At each center where students were seen they discussed the growing ease of female applicants in confronting male faculty about inappropriate comments. Students of both sexes confirmed these observations of the assertiveness of individual women. In addition, women as a group are less likely to allow offensive attitudes to go unheeded. Perhaps a direct result of their more assertive behavior is the interviewers' heightened sensitivity to these issues.

Both women and men students in all the centers visited think questions relating to the dual careers of family and profession are important, but they should be discussed with candidates of both sexes. They suggest that the questions per se are usually not offensive if kept to general subjects such as marriage and family. They do object, however, if queries force communication with a stranger about personal concerns such as dating patterns or the use of birth control measures. There was surprising unanimity in the responses of female and male students concerning appropriate, uniform interviewing of all candidates. This is an area where it is difficult to know whether societal change has encouraged male peer support of women, or whether the rise in the number of women has had this effect.

Members of admissions committees report there have been alterations in the structure of their committees over the last ten years; for example, most now include female faculty members, and while their numbers are usually small in proportion to the number of men, this is more a reflection of the low percentage of women on medical school faculties; some committees have both female and male student members. The presence of both women faculty and students of both sexes has resulted in the raising of consciousness of other committee members about concerns unique to women applicants, and, indeed, has broadened the discussion of other major issues.

The question remains as to which came first in the schools visited: the admission of more women or the inclusion of females on admissions committees. At Stanford there is a group concerned about the future of women in medicine. The project was funded by the Macy Foundation in 1967, and in the spring of 1969 a group called Professional Women at Stanford Medical School was formed. The rise in the number of women accepted at Stanford Medical Center began in the late 1960s. In December 1970 the Joint Committee on the Status and Tenure of Women proposed to the Stanford Faculty Senate that the medical school set an objective of expanding the enrollment of female students. Thus the women already at that medical school launched an effort to enlarge their applicant pool; the data available show they succeeded in doing so.

Medical school classes are more heterogeneous today than in the 1960s. Davis Johnson wrote in 1975:

> . . . I would characterize them [medical students in 1975] as being not only greater in quantity but also better in academic quality and much more diverse in sex and racial background, than their counterparts of even four short years ago.[12]

This is due in part to admissions policies and in part to federal legislation. Marital status, for example, can no longer be asked on preadmission forms, according to Title IX of the Federal Education Amendments and Titles VII and VIII of the Public Health Service Act. This prohibition is added to the longstanding ones concerning questions about a candidate's race, religion, creed, color, or national origin.

Policies about accepting older candidates vary with the institution. In general, medical colleges consider the application of older persons of either sex with skepticism. If they have worked in a health-related field or have a special reason for wanting to pursue a medical education, special consideration may be given to such individual applicants.[13] When there is a choice between two equally qualified candidates, one directly out of college and the other an older individual, the committee is likely to choose the former, for it is generally thought that the younger student has the promise of a greater number of productive years. Thus in most schools decisions about older students are related to age rather than sex.

Several individuals on admissions committees note that the decisions are made by the group, and on most committees no one member's veto can deter acceptance of a qualified individual. One member's bias against a woman on the basis of her sex, therefore, would be overridden by the will of the majority. Most members state they are truly interested in the best qualified student, regardless of sex, race, or marital status. None of the schools visited has a quota system for females.

One institution's female students questioned this statement of fairness to all candidates when they compared the classes of 1978 and 1979, which record a decrement of 9 percent in the enrollment of women (Table 8). Admissions committee officials and students are going over these data carefully. For most schools, however, the percentage of women enrolled increased during the early 1970s, and may now be plateauing as applications from women have leveled off. Because there is variation from year to year in individual schools, the overall data for the nation are more meaningful than data from individual institutions.

Role Models

In most medical schools in the 1960s there were few females to serve as role models for women medical students. That situation has not changed for the better, and may even be

Table 8. Admissions Data (School C)

Class of	Total Applications	Female Applications	Percent	Total Class	Females in Class	Percent
1972	1,009	97	10	47	8	18
1974	2,361	379	16	57	11	19
1976	3,434	563	16	65	15	23
1978	4,096	915	22	96	21	21
1979	4,132	1,005	24	96	12	12

worse. In 1965–66, 15 percent of the faculty in seventy-eight of the existing eighty-nine medical schools in the United States were women; in 1975 the percentage was 9.9 (Table 9).[14, 15]

The issue of role models for students of both sexes is a broader one than the availability of female physicians who may be contacted by female students. When asked to define an ideal role model, one group of students of both sexes said the ideal should be a person who is sensitive to his/her patients; knows his/her specialty and can teach it to students; and, especially for women, is married, has a family, and in general is regarded positively by students.

Most women and men agree that the sex of the role model is inconsequential, except for a few female students who specifically want to relate to a female physician. Students complain that in the medical schools, where most physicians teach, do research, and carry on minimal patient care in comparison to their practicing colleagues, it is difficult to find excellent role models. Many of today's doctors-in-training, particularly preclinical students, say they ultimately want to go into primary care, and question the relevance of an ongoing personal contact with academicians. It appears, therefore, that both male and female students find the availability of relevant role models a problem.

The accessibility of female role models for those medical students who seek them is a perplexing situation at institutions where there are few women faculty members. At others, even

Table 9. Faculty in United States Medical Schools
Holding Medical Degrees

Year	Men	Women	
		Number	Percent
1965–66[a]	14,522	2,112	15.0
1975[b]	23,923	2,623	9.9

SOURCE: Carol Lopate, *Women in Medicine* (Baltimore: Johns Hopkins Press for the Josiah Macy, Jr. Foundation, 1968); and H. Paul Jolly and Thomas A. Larson, *Participation of Women and Minorities on U.S. Medical School Faculties* (Washington: Association of American Medical Colleges, 1976).
  [a] Figures are for seventy-eight of the eighty-nine existing medical schools.
  [b] Figures are for all 116 existing medical schools.

though there are a number of women on the faculty, their relevance and their availability to students are often in question. Direct quotes from students in one center that has several female faculty members are:

- There are a few females, but their style is far too different from mine to make it useful. I have been formally exposed to about four female doctors—about one lecture each. I think this is a lousy situation and a major problem.
- If I made the effort I could probably find one, but the amount of free time prevents me from doing so.
- I have been told they are around. I just don't know who they are or how to contact them.

In some academic medical centers women faculty are accessible, relevant, and known to the students, but they are in the minority in the institutions visited.

Today's students, particularly clinical clerks, find the female house staff more understanding than some female faculty. They sometimes think older faculty are not conscious of the rapid societal change that has affected their lifestyles. In addition, because of the growing number of women at the student–house staff level, there are more female house officers than female faculty. Surgery and obstetrics and gynecology, particularly, have few female faculty representatives, but a greater number of house staff. Thus the increasing number of women at this level has shifted some of the responsibility for role models from the faculty to the house staff.

Preclinical students of both sexes often do not know who to seek out as a role model. In some medical schools there are first-year/fourth-year student tutorial programs that in the judgment of students work well, for the young student may rely on his/her fourth-year tutor for guidance in seeking information about faculty–house staff role models. Again, more women medical students than faculty participate in the tutorials—another example of how the influx of women has changed medical center activities.

Nonphysician females in administration or related health fields serve as role models for some women students; other students seek role models outside medicine. This may become less likely as a greater variety of women physicians become available within the medical centers.

Supportive Services

Academic Advisors. Some medical schools assign faculty advisors to medical students, a system that works well at some institutions but not at others. Many of the schools visited had well-established programs; at others the systems were minimally functional or nonexistent. The advisor-advisee relationship often grows in response to common research or clinical interests, or to other, nonmedical interests.

In terms of advisory considerations, the same issues are important to both female and male students. In answer to the question, "Are there special advisory considerations for women in your institution?", one woman wrote, "Why should there be?" Another woman at the same school wrote, "Are they necessary? I have found the faculty more than sympathetic to me as a woman." The majority feel there is no reason to prospectively pair a woman advisor and a female student.

Another concern of students of both sexes is that they should be able to select their own advisors. Where the student has a choice, if a woman student wants a female advisor her wishes could be accommodated; if a woman student seeks a male advisor or a male student a female advisor, this, too, would be possible. The student's freedom to choose an advisor facilitates communication.

The question of the desirability of a "dean of women" was raised with students and administrators. Even though some women thought there should be a designated dean for women, the majority of students and administrators agreed that a special dean for women was not a necessity, and that to appoint one would perhaps serve to separate women from the current system rather than to integrate them into the existing administrative structure. Whether there should be women deans with broad assignments in the medical school dean's office, is another question. There are students of both sexes who agree that the recruitment for openings in a dean's office should include consideration of skilled women and men, and that the most qualified candidate should get the job; others believe that, since there are so few women in the administrative offices of the nation's medical schools, every effort should be made through affirmative action to see that women are recruited to open positions.

The fact that the issues of advisory systems for women and the appointment of women deans are even being considered, and were discussed easily in each setting visited, suggests another development in the medical schools, secondary to the expanding number of women.

Counseling Services. In some schools there are identified faculty or staff to whom the student can turn for advice on personal problems. In one medical school where there is a dearth of female faculty, the registrar, a female nonphysician, is the person the students prefer to go to when they need assistance. At other institutions where there are more women physicians, certain women are identified as being very helpful. The 1975 "Report of the Student Task Force (HMS) of the Joint Committee on the Status of Women" presents data from a questionnaire distributed to women students asking for "the names of any individuals at Harvard who have been helpful to you in the area of career advising or personal advising or both." The names most often listed are included in the summary of that report.[16]

Some medical schools have counseling centers for students. Where such facilities exist, students state it is crucial that they be told exactly how to go about getting help: the services may be very good, but students may be unaware of them. Several university health services provide comprehensive health care, including counseling for students.[17] Many students of both sexes, particularly in the smaller schools, seek consultation with professionals outside the medical center, even though specific services are available at the school, so that those individuals who will ultimately judge their students' academic performance will not have access to their personal histories. Such outside professionals include doctors, clergymen, social workers, and psychologists.

Most students of both sexes agree there should be identified women counselors to whom female students may go if they so choose. At Harvard Medical School, women members of the Joint Committee on the Status of Women are known by the medical students and are available for consultation. Some of the issues women students want to discuss with other females are: women in medicine; the female as a medical student and the stresses she may encounter from time to time; the multiple roles of a woman in medicine – doctor, wife, and mother.

Groups for women medical students exist in several schools. Elaine Hilberman notes that:

> A number of authors suggest the importance of a support system for women students in order to provide role models and opportunities for mutual sharing and solving of problems, but the availability of such support is rare. . . . Their feelings of isolation in medical school, anxiety about course demands, and anger over sex discrimination were aired, shared, and in part resolved, at times, by establishing new friendships, discussing mutual fears, or actively protesting biased behavior. Professional identity was developed and enhanced. . . . It should, however, be firmly stated that role conflicts are not peculiar to women professionals. Male classmates of the women group participants frequently expressed their own need for a similar program.[18]

A member of the University Health Service at Harvard Medical School has organized a group of ten second-year women students; the major purposes of participation are to decrease the sense of isolation; to allow students to become acquainted with one another; and to share mutual concerns.*

There should be a variety of counseling services for both female and male students. In the last decade some improvements have been made in the development of appropriate services for women: in addition to the formation of groups, some university health services are considering better care for women; and individual faculty, female and male, are increasing their awareness of the needs of women students. It is again

---

* Roberta Apfel Savitz, 1976: personal communication.

difficult to state that these innovations have come about solely because there are more women in the medical centers, but data suggest that they are responsible for a conscious awareness of the concerns of women on the parts of others. More must be done in this area, however.

Activities of Daily Living

This section will consider the interpersonal contacts of female students with their peers of both sexes; faculty-women student interactions; on-call and leisure facilities for women students; and marital status. Each is an area where some women encountered problems in the 1960s; other women who were medical students at that time denied that these issues were of major concern.

There is a mixed picture in the 1970s—some improvement in the activities of daily living for some women; less for others. Some state they continue to experience major problems in peer and faculty communication.

Peer Communication. The problems of an individual woman student vary according to the nature of the specific interaction experienced with a peer or faculty member; her awareness of women's issues; and the sensitivity of the particular student. These are highly complex areas, and drawing generalizations is hardly justified.

In general, women students in the schools visited report that their male peers are very supportive. For example, some men accompany women students to express their consternation to a professor over the presentation of materials offensive to females. Many of the men said their female classmates have raised their level of consciousness about women's issues, and thus have contributed to their own education. Some males, similar to some in the mid-1800s who were dedicated to the cause of the Women's Movement, have made quite an investment in the cause of women, beyond a passing concern about male faculty-female interaction.

Not all male-female peer interactions are pleasant, however. A minority of women students interviewed report that some of their male classmates do not treat them as equals; one said that one of her male peers insisted on calling her "nurse" throughout their clinical rotation. One second-year male student told of the tension that existed between first-year women and men in his school. He reported that by the second year these feelings had disappeared. The following excerpt appeared in one medical school's newspaper: "We need a few good men to do a man's job—If that doesn't recruit a few women, I don't know what will." This statement might be interpreted as humorous by some women; others would find it offensive. There are examples in almost every medical school of communications that are offensive to a female recipient. Improvement is being made in this area, however.

In general, women students are supported by their female peers, but the degree of support varies. In some schools women believe they have common goals and interests and are mutually supportive. As the number of women students grows, and as more are married while still in medical school, the necessity for female camaraderie may decrease. The need to stay together as a minority will lessen as they are given more support by their male colleagues.

Faculty Communication. Interactions of women medical students with male faculty vary. Male professors, in general, treat women and men students with equal fairness. Most medical centers, however, include some male faculty who do not. "Obstacles to Equal Education at Harvard Resulting from Sex Discrimination" records several ways in which faculty discriminate against women medical students:

> A. *Condescension.* . . . calling a woman student "dear," "gal," or by her first name when male colleagues are called Mr. or Dr. is a frequent form of condescension.
> B. *Hostility.* . . . an instructor beginning a lecture on genetics drew "XXXX" on the blackboard and then commented, "The more female you get, the more retarded you are."
> C. *Role Stereotyping.* " . . . why don't you stay home and have babies?"[19]

Students agree that these interpersonal misfortunes occur more frequently on the clinical services than in the preclinical years. Interactions on the clinical service are closer, one professor to one student, rather than one teacher to many students; clinical medicine focuses closely on the basic issues of life, which involve multiple stresses; and the tradition in American medicine has been one of an authoritarian relationship, with the physician as a father figure and the student, particularly the woman, the passive recipient of his directives. Flirtatious behavior between a male professor and a female student may be considered "cute" in some settings, but serious women students usually do not perceive it as such in the clinical setting. The majority of female students observe that when they have the support of sympathetic male or female classmates on a clinical rotation, the special attention accorded females by some male mentors often disappears. Students report they are observing less of this chauvinistic behavior in the medical schools.

Consistently reported in several settings were communication problems between male faculty and female students in hospitals where there have until recently been few female students, in comparison with university hospitals where more women are visible. Students think that as more women students and physicians work together in the hospital setting, conditions will improve. This, then, is one area where students find that the increasing female presence is having an effect on the behavior of male faculty.

In addition to male faculty-female student interactions, women professors' attitudes toward students of their own sex should be noted. Female students report that some female faculty are fair; others are described as being unsupportive, sometimes hostile, and in general insensitive to the students' specific needs. One noted educator described the dynamics of this process as being similar to that of the battered child syndrome: often the parents themselves were battered children. Correspondingly, some women faculty have achieved success in medicine despite working in a system that did not support their progress. In their opinion today's young women also must prove themselves and experience the same kinds of difficulties. This phenomenon is related to the strong belief of older women doctors that they all had to excel, so that women in medicine, as a group, would not be degraded. One female full professor at a leading university hospital summed up her feelings by expressing relief over the expanding numbers of women in the medical schools, because it means that for any one woman the pressure to shoulder the responsibility for all women will not be so great. She said she now relaxes and enjoys the female students in her classes, for no longer as their professor must she help them prove their worth. This is another specific example of how the presence of more female students is changing faculty behavior.

The rise in the number of female medical students has improved the awareness of most of their male peers and professors in some respects. Discrimination, when it occurs, is less likely to be overt; it may be subtle, and thus more difficult to document. Women professors should explore their feelings about the growing number of women entering medicine and serve as advocates for their young colleagues. Still more work must be done to educate faculty and students about these issues.

Facilities. There is great variation in the adequacy of on-call facilities for women students; in some institutions they are poor for both women and men. Differences within some hospitals vary according to the particular clinical service. In order to gain an understanding of on-call facilities at the institutions visited, it would have been necessary to see every clinical service and every teaching site, which was impossible. Therefore these data at best are general.

One problem that affects both men and women is forced, integrated sleeping quarters, necessitated by lack of space and greater numbers of trainees of both sexes. At one institution a male resident and female intern were assigned the only remaining on-call room. The man said this was a problem for him; the woman said it was not one for her. He then suggested she might sleep elsewhere — that is, outside in the corridor. She said she wouldn't, so he slept outside! Men as well as women may be personally offended by such arrangements.

On some services the number or adequacy of sleeping quarters is discrepant: women are given the poorer accommodations. Some institutions are remodeling their facilities to adjust to the influx of women; others are not, claiming that fiscal and architectural limitations do not allow them to do so.

Women in still male-dominated surgical suites complain constantly about having to shower and change in nurses' dressing rooms. In some hospitals women have to enter the male changing area in order to obtain surgical pants, if they prefer them to dresses. At one newly constructed hospital, women house officers have to traverse a door to the male bathroom before entering their on-call rooms. In these instances, the increase in the number of women house officers has had little demonstrable effect on tradition.

Satisfactory leisure facilities for both men and women are often not available. Occasionally there are complaints that the men's quarters have a more accessible shower or are closer to the medical center, but by and large where adequate facilities do exist they are open to both sexes.

Women and men face similar problems in certain institutions with regard to on-call and leisure facilities, but for women the difficulties in these areas are greater. The strength of feelings on these issues depends on the individual student and the inadequacy of the facility.

Marital Status. There is greater diversity in the composition of student bodies today than in the 1960s. In some classes there are older married women who enter medical school after their children are in school; there are also one-parent families, where the woman or man is single, separated, or divorced. Options are greater today for the unmarried older woman than ten years ago. Academic faculties seem to have accepted the change in the status of their students without major problems.

Consideration of the issues of marriage, family, and career are of great importance to women medical students today — most state they would like to marry and combine a career with raising a family. Serious concern is expressed during the medical school years as to how women in the past handled these major responsibilities simultaneously. Contact with successful women doctors who are doing both is important. It is interesting to note that men are also concerned about many of these same issues.

Childbearing, childrearing, and attending medical school

simultaneously present many difficulties. Some women design schedules to accommodate their own and their families' needs, but, with increasing responsibility to both family and medical school, this may be a burden. The University of Hawaii is experimenting with a flexible program, as are other institutions. If more schools adopt less rigid schedules, this will reflect another area of improvement. Whether this is occurring as secondary to societal change or because of pressure from women, again, is hard to document.

For a young woman physician to cope successfully with family responsibilities, she needs a supportive, flexible spouse and dependable help—a live-in housekeeper, a day-care center, or a baby-sitter. The majority of women choose not to have children until after they graduate from medical school, however. (The issue of day care will be examined in the faculty section, see page 42.)

Loneliness and social isolation are major problems for the single female medical student for whom socialization both within and outside the medical center is important. Group activities may facilitate communication for these women.

Faculty

> The current situation has become more favorable for female faculty members in view of the pressure for more women in faculty positions; hence the increase of women on faculty committees. Professionally, things have improved, and this has become a time for women to be welcomed and accepted professionally. For the most part personal discrimination is melting away.
>
> Female assistant professor

Overview

Several federal laws prohibit discrimination against individuals on academic faculties on the basis of sex. The major laws documented by A.E. Bayer and H.S. Astin include:[20]

- *Executive Order 11246,* as amended by 11375, which prohibits discrimination in employment (including hiring, salaries, fringe benefits, training, upgrading, and other conditions of employment) on the basis of sex and certain other factors, and requires an affirmative action plan.

• *Title VII of the Civil Rights Act of 1964,* as amended by the Equal Employment Opportunity Act of 1972, prohibits discrimination in academic employment.

• Equal Pay Act of 1963, as amended by the Education Amendments of 1972 (Higher Education Act), prohibits discrimination in salaries and covers nonacademic as well as academic employees.

• *Title IX of the Education Amendments of 1972* reaffirms the compliance regulations of the earlier orders, extends coverage to part-time employees, and requires that equal pensions be determined for men and women employees.

Legislative and societal developments over the last decade have resulted in a rise in the number of women serving on medical school faculties. Thus, for the faculty, this situation has not come about solely because of the pressure caused by the influx of women. In fact the ratio of women faculty members remains low, as a direct reflection of the paucity of women medical students prior to the 1960s. Despite an overall improvement in salaries, promotion, and tenure in some academic centers, discrepancies still remain between salary levels and ease of promotion for individual women in comparison to their male colleagues. Ideal solutions to combining family and professional responsibilities have still not been defined. The problems unmarried women doctors experience are, however, being clarified.

Number of Women on Faculties and Specialty Choices

In the 1965–66 academic year there were 2,112 women and 14,522 men on the faculties of seventy-eight of the eighty-nine United States medical schools; women thus accounted for 15 percent of the total.[21] In 1976 the Association of American Medical Colleges (AAMC) reported that 2,623 women and 23,923 men were on medical school faculties as of 31 December 1975: the percentage of women had fallen to 9.9 percent

(Table 9). The largest numbers of women were appointed in departments of pediatrics, anesthesiology, physical medicine, public health, pathology, obstetrics and gynecology, psychiatry, and radiology (Table 10).[22]

The majority of female faculty members interviewed said they would have entered specialties other than those they were in if the opportunities had existed when they chose their internships. At one leading medical school, for example, a woman recalled that ten years ago as a senior medical student she discussed her excellent progress in internal medicine with the chairman of that department. While he recognized the superiority of her record, he said she could not apply for an internship in that department because no women were admitted to the program. She never questioned his decision and entered pediatrics. In the early 1960s another woman bravely entered an internship in obstetrics and gynecology, a field in which there were few, if any, female physicians at the time. She did not know whether she could progress to the residency, even though all her male colleagues had decided on their futures. She completed her training, but was never able to plan ahead for more than one year at a time. Her response in discussing this situation fifteen years later was, "I had to work

Table 10. Men and Women Medical Faculty by Department
(As of 31 December 1975)

Department	Men	Women	Percent of Women
Pediatrics	2,088	695	25
Anesthesiology	943	219	19
Physical medicine	249	52	17
Public health/preventive medicine	398	65	14
Pathology	1,683	229	12
Obstetrics and gynecology	1,050	122	10
Psychiatry	2,477	277	10
Radiology	1,586	183	10
Medicine	6,203	464	7
Administration	300	11	4
Orthopedic surgery	304	6	2
Surgery	3,202	65	2

SOURCE: H. Paul Jolly and Thomas A. Larson, *Participation of Women and Minorities in U.S. Medical School Faculties* (Washington: Association of American Medical Colleges, 1976).

hard and not make any waves." She is currently serving on that university's faculty.

Today's women faculty members chose their specialties at least ten years ago; almost all specialties are now open to qualified young women. (See section on house staff page 45.)

Women in Administration

While a few more women hold administrative positions in medical schools today compared to ten years ago, there are still no full-time women deans (Table 11).[23] Under the pressure of affirmative action, however, some medical schools have recently named women as associate or assistant deans. Harvard Medical School will soon have three women departmental chairmen; other schools have a scattering of such appointments. It will probably be some time before any significant number of women hold decision-making positions in academic medical centers. Again, these changes will probably be related more to federal action than to the growing numbers of women in the centers.

Salaries

The Equal Pay Act of 1963, as amended by the 1972 Higher Education Act, which covers nonacademic and academic employees, prohibits discrimination in salaries. It has long been

Table 11. Women Deans Holding Medical Degrees in
114 United States Medical Schools

	Full	Associate	Assistant
Total number	121	257	127
Number of positions held by women	0	8	8
Percentage held by women	0	3.1	6.3

SOURCE: M. H. Witte, A. J. Arem, and M. Holguin, "Women Physicians in United States Medical Schools: Preliminary Report," *Journal of the American Medical Women's Association* 31 (1976): 211.

recognized that salaries of women in academia are on the average less than those of men in similar posts. In 1968–69, according to Bayer and Astin:

> An average raise for women of more than $1,000 across all ranks would have been required for equity in accordance with the predictors of men's salaries. The comparable figure in 1972–73 was $600. . . . equity in salary between men and women has been virtually achieved in the junior ranks while differentials persist in the senior ranks, particularly at the level of full professor.[24]

One medical center reported that the annual differential in salary between male and female professionals in 1974–75 was $1,056.[25]

A greater equity of salaries has evolved in the last decade. Even though there appears to be improvement in salary levels for women as a group, however, individual females may be offered and accept a lower salary than their male peers. A class-action suit has been filed by a woman faculty member against a southern university in response to alleged discrimination in women's salaries and promotions; the case is pending.[26]

When women physicians were asked about their salaries compared to men of equal status, two replied:

● Low. Usually in a poor position to argue, because [I] want [a] job.

● When my potential chairman knew my husband was staying on the faculty, he offered me a considerably lower salary for the job for which I applied than I thought I deserved. With the possibility that I might go to another medical center in town, an equitable salary was offered me.

These quotes illustrate the difficulties women still experience in salary negotiations in the medical centers. If a woman physician has a specialty that can be practiced only in one setting in the city where she and her family live she may have no alternative but to accept the salary offered, as noted by the woman first quoted. To make too big an issue of her departmental chairman's decision about her income may mean losing the job. In the second example the woman had other options, stated them, and received a salary appropriate to her level. That she questioned the original salary offer indicates that the chairman was trying to recruit her for as low a sum as possible.

Other women faculty report they are satisfied with their salaries because the family has another source of income — the husband's — and so the women do not worry about their own being inequitable. As more unmarried women begin to serve on medical school faculties, the salary issue may become more serious, as those women may have no other source of income. Thus pressure from the growing number of single women may, in the future, support the changes already mandated by federal legislation.

Most women report they benefit from having a senior advocate in the system, preferably male, to negotiate directly with deans or chairmen about their salaries. Women faculty with such advocacy have probably consistently done better than their counterparts who lack such support.

It is becoming harder for an institution to justify such large discrepancies in the salaries of females and males, for it may lose federal funds if such inequities continue.

Promotion and Tenure

In many academic institutions women are given promotions and tenure less quickly than their male colleagues. This is a very difficult area to assess, as criteria for promotion may vary from one institution to another. In addition, part-time women faculty may not be as productive by university criteria as their full-time male peers. Women faculty experience several problems in this regard: some assume large patient-care loads, often to the exclusion of research activities; some, realizing that they may not be rewarded by promotion and tenure at the same rate as their full-time, research-oriented male colleagues, make a conscious decision to concentrate on direct patient care, thus delaying their promotions. Others practice patient care without recognizing that their work will be minimally rewarded in an academic setting. They may be drawn to patient care because it gives them satisfaction, or because a chairman overtly or covertly encourages them to do so. They become aware of the criteria for promotion and tenure only when the questions arise. Many of these women feel they would have proceeded differently if they had known what was expected of them.

Another major drawback for women doing part-time research is that their research productivity and their academic progress may take a longer time than those of their male peers. Considerable thought is now being given to the development of an alternate timetable for promoting women physicians who are raising children, so that they will not be penalized because it takes them longer to become as productive as their full-time male collegues.

Some individual women express dissatisfaction with their experience regarding promotions, whereas others are satisfied. One female faculty member, who had access to information on faculty being considered for promotion and tenure, maintains there is still evidence of discrimination in this area in her institution.

One of the major disadvantages women experienced in the past was their lack of mobility if they were unable to negotiate equitable terms for promotion. Ten years ago a married woman physician with children often felt she had to stay in the location where her spouse was employed. But society is changing, and women now recognize that moving to a position at another medical center is possible for them as well as for their husbands. There have been recent examples of entire families relocating because the woman had been offered a more promising opportunity, thus necessitating her husband's seeking employment compatible with hers. This change in mobility status is a societal issue, which does not seem related to the increasing number of women in the medical centers. Society ultimately affects what transpires in the medical center, however.

Some academicians are concerned that affirmative action will result in unqualified women being promoted or assuming senior administrative roles. The promotion of an individual with inadequate qualifications encourages a self-fulfilling prophecy of failure; in addition, it will offend women who have struggled for equity with men. Elizabeth Drouilhet, on retiring from a long career at Vassar College, expressed this sentiment very well:

> I believe in equal rights for all individuals, regardless of sex. I believe in equal pay and equal reward for the same service performed, for all individuals regardless of sex. I believe that the best qualified person should be selected for the job to be done, regardless of sex. Women have fought hard and won the right to be judged on their qualifications and merit. I cringe every time I hear the sentence, "that job, or that anything, must go to a woman." It is an insult to all the women who have fought valiantly for equality — their fight was for the right to be equally considered and judged, not to be handed something because of their sex.[27]

Profession and Family

The problem reported in the *Philadelphia Medical Times* has changed little since 1871:

> We learn on what seems to be good authority that the "leading lady" . . . of the (female) medical profession in London is going to take unto herself a husband. Questions of interest come up in such a case. Will the lady continue to practice medicine and her husband follow his own occupation? And if so, and the union should prove prolific, who will train up their offspring in the way they should do?[28]

Today approximately 80 percent of women doctors are married; 50 percent marry physicians.[29] For the woman who chooses the combination of an academic career, marriage, and a family, several dilemmas exist: it is difficult for a young physician/mother to pursue academia full time and bear and rear her children; some work full time and spend only minimal time on child-care responsibilities; others work part time; and still others drop out of academic work and return at a later date. Ultimately, all will be judged academically on standards set for the research productivity of a full-time person. This picture has changed little in the last decade.

A recent article draws a comparison between the career timetable of full-time academic males and the average age of career attainments for females who take five years off at one point in their careers because of family responsibilities: in Pattern I, a woman takes five years off after the completion of her residency; in Pattern II, five years off prior to entering medical school; and in Pattern III, five years off between the assistant and associate professor levels (Table 12).[30] More studies should be undertaken to devise alternate career patterns for females who must take time off to be with their families. This is an example of how larger numbers of women

Table 12. Sample Career Patterns—Average Age on Attainment of Career Milestones

	Male Candidates	Female Candidates		
		Pattern I	Pattern II	Pattern III
Entry to medical school	21	21	26 *	21
Graduation from medical school	25	25	30	25
Completion of residency	28	28 *	33	28
Completion of fellowship	31	36	36	31
Assistant professor	31[a]	36	36	31
Chair—regional AFCR[b] session	34	39	39	38 *
Associate professor	36	41	41	40
Chair—national AFCR session	36	—	—	—
Councilor, AFCR	35–36	ineligible	ineligible	ineligible
Division head	38	—	—	—
Tenure	39	44	44	43
Senior member, AFCR	41	41	41	41

SOURCE: E. M. Short, "Women in the AFCR: Present Status and Future Prospects," *Clinical Research* 24 (1976): 124.

* Five years, during which a substantial portion of time is devoted to family responsibilities.

[a] Fellowship often includes military service; if not, candidate may be age thirty-two at appointment to assistant professor.

[b] American Federation for Clinical Research.

on faculties in the future may force modifications to be made in traditional career patterns.

Many women have found ways to combine productive academic careers and family responsibilities. Some have arranged to work part time and have remained productive by university standards by minimizing clinical work and concentrating on a single academic field. One woman who chose a particular area of lung pathology has become an expert in that field. Another works full time and keeps regular daytime hours devoted mostly to clinical work. She is home with her young family from 6 until 10 P.M., and then returns to the medical center to finish up the day's work and pursue academic activities. The latter example is the exception rather than the rule, but it does show that it is possible for a woman who is motivated to fulfill family and professional commitments. Thus, to date, compromises around the issues of family and career have been made by the woman physician; they have not come about from changes in the medical centers' attitudes.

A young mother may find that the demands of her academic position and her children's needs for her peak simultaneously. A myth exists that once a youngster is one to two years of age it is less dependent on the mother. Indeed, the opposite may be true: for a woman who bears children when she is in her late twenties and early thirties, the children may become more demanding as her academic responsibilities grow.

A supportive spouse willing to share some household responsibilities is of paramount importance to the working mother. Three successful married women physicians report the following about their husbands:

- Very helpful and supportive.
- Shares household chores on practically a fifty-fifty basis.
- Excellent. If not, the combination would be impossible.

Some women who lack this support separate or sue for divorce.

The fact that there are more women in the medical centers has had little effect on this dilemma. There are not yet enough faculty women to force consideration of alternatives. Most young women interviewed are struggling with their personal resolution of continuing to combine marriage and a career.

Child Care

Few university medical centers in the United States have adequate child-care facilities. It is recognized that sustained action is necessary to produce a viable program of day care. Unfortunately, mothers frequently lose interest in day care as their children outgrow the need. A new group of young mothers then begins to work on the problem, and its resolution is again postponed for years.

Most faculty women say they can afford child care, either on a daily or a live-in basis. Availability of adequate mother substitutes may be limited, however, and this is a major concern. In some settings the wives of medical students take care of faculty children, to the satisfaction of both parties. A survey conducted by the American Medical Women's Association reported that inadequate household help was a major deterrent to women who want to remain productive.[31] Even in households where help is satisfactory, prolonged illness or absence of the housekeeper may mean the mother loses work time.

Several suggestions about child care by female faculty warrant consideration:

1. There should be a tax deduction for live-in help. Despite adequate, often double, incomes in homes where both parents are professionals, live-in help is expensive, and for some prohibitive, without tax relief.

2. Quality hospital- or university-based day care is needed in many medical centers. Women whose children are currently being cared for during the day usually must rely on community facilities.

3. There should be greater communication among faculty women and men and a sharing of knowledge about the availability of child-care facilities in a given geographic area. This approach could be accomplished through meetings at certain levels in a department, for example, informal meetings of assistant professors, or meetings of groups of senior physicians and younger women doctors.

Again, the major difficulty is that the number of faculty

women is still so small in most settings that the child-care issues go unresolved.

Other Issues

Minority Faculty Women. At a conference on minority women scientists in December 1975, several observations were made:

1. If the pool of minority women scientists is to be enlarged, vigorous leadership will be needed at the highest administrative levels in public and private institutions.

2. The participants strongly opposed the double counting system, by which employers count minority women twice, thus distorting statistics to escape their obligations to hire more minorities and women.

3. The women scientists objected to systems which . . . often penalized and rarely rewarded them for engaging in activities specifically designed to address the exclusion of minorities and/or women from training and careers. . .[32]

Unmarried Women. Remaining single is the conscious choice of some of today's young women. They do not experience the conflict of career versus family, but they frequently have other problems, such as social isolation in the medical center. They are often seen by their married colleagues as pursuing a more masculine route to their career—in some cases devoting full time to their profession. They may be excluded from social gatherings because they are unmarried. Isolation as an issue may be disappearing as society changes, however, and the motivated woman will find opportunities for contacts outside the medical center and through travel.

Females recently separated or divorced may find it difficult to be a single parent and a professional simultaneously. The personal stress of recent separation or divorce, in addition to the burden of rearing children alone, may be a hardship for a woman physician.

Overutilization. Women who are struggling for promotion and tenure are being asked to serve on too many committees.

Senior faculty women feel more secure about declining such invitations, but those at lower faculty levels often feel they must accept. Committee work adds little to academic progress in most institutions, and thus the woman is placed in a position of conflict: she wants to be on the committees to represent the interests of women, but she needs the time to become productive academically. Thus the pressure to include more women on most committees may be a burden on the few women who are on medical faculties.

Comment

Some women in medical centers have joined together to communicate, plan, and document specific problems faced by women in the centers. An example of this approach is the Joint Committee on the Status of Women at Harvard—a standing committee in the Harvard Medical School area. Several pamphlets it has put out have highlighted women's concerns in that setting and have helped to raise the level of consciousness of other members of the medical school community.

Other universities, the University of California at Irvine (UCI), for example, are forming similar groups. At UCI, twenty-four-hour day care, maternity-paternity leave up to one year, and official review of files for inappropriate and/or discriminatory comments are being studied.

Thus, as more women move into the medical centers, the need is greater to join together to define common goals and provide mutual support. Approximately half the institutions visited either have or are contemplating such groups.

House Staff

I feel that in the years since I started medical school [1970] the atmosphere has changed considerably, as I have, too! The subtle jabs against women are much less frequent, though they still occur. The increasing number of women makes us much more visible, and also demythifies us, letting each of us be treated as just a person more of the time.

First-year female resident

Overview

There have been marked developments in house officer training opportunities for women physicians in the last decade. The steady rise in the numbers of women accepted into medical school in the early 1970s is being reflected in an increment in the corps of female house staff. A major change has occurred in the accessibility of training programs in surgery and internal medicine. Some centers are developing flexible residency programs that allow trainees to extend their period of training, thus creating a less intensive pace than in the past. This mode of training is as yet available only on a limited basis, however.

Problems connected with child care still exist for the young mother-physician. In comparison with her faculty counterpart, who may work shorter hours and who can afford adequate help, the young house officer often works long, irregular hours and may not be able to pay for good child care.

As more women enter fields where heretofore they have been underrepresented, they must help their skeptical male colleagues understand that qualified women can meet the challenge and do the job. In settings where this has occurred, women are welcomed on the house staff. The young woman of today may face minimal barriers in medical school, a different experience than her counterpart of ten years ago, but she may be poorly prepared to cope with unwelcoming attitudes during her postgraduate years.

Women in Residencies and Specialty Choices

A total of 2,902 American and Canadian women house officers were enrolled in training programs in 1974, compared to 1,419 in 1968.[33,34] Popular choices for women are pediatrics, internal medicine, psychiatry, and pathology (Table 13). More women entered family medicine, obstetrics and gynecology, and general surgery in 1974 than ever before.[35–37]

In one study conducted at two university medical centers, family medicine was the most popular specialty for both sexes: almost half the females (44 percent) selected family practice as

Table 13. Women Resident Physicians by Specialty
(United States and Canadian Graduates)

Specialty	1968	Per-cent	1970	Per-cent	1974	Per-cent
Anesthesiology	99	7.0	72	4.0	107	3.7
Family practice	–		8	0.4	133	4.6
General practice	5	0.4	–		–	
General surgery	65	4.6	95	5.3	187	6.4
Internal medicine	239	16.8	290	16.3	534	18.4
Obstetrics and gynecology	80	5.6	76	4.3	167	5.8
Pathology	120	8.4	138	7.8	184	6.3
Pediatrics	246	17.3	354	20.0	595	20.5
Psychiatry, including child	326	23.0	411	23.0	482	16.6
Radiology	82	5.8	137	7.7	157	5.4
Others	157	11.0	197	11.0	356	12.3
Total	1,419	99.9	1,778	99.8	2,902	100.0

SOURCE: *Journal of the American Medical Association* 210 (1969): 1553; 218 (1971): 1250; 234 (1975): 1365. Copyright 1969, 1971, 1975, American Medical Association.

their first choice. Pediatrics was the second choice for women; internal medicine for men. Surgery was the third choice for men; the last for the women. Women believed internal medicine was highest in status; men thought surgery was first.[38]

Women are freer to apply for enrollment in male-dominated specialties than were their colleagues a decade or more ago. Some programs that previously had few or no women are now aggressively seeking qualified women. Thus the increase in women graduating from medical school has probably served to open up nontraditional specialties to them. The rise in the number who successfully go through training programs that previously excluded females should serve to encourage training directors to continue to take well-qualified women as house officers.

Flexible Residencies

The house officer experience demands almost total devotion to duty. Today, however, both female and male house staff are questioning whether they want to pursue their training on a full-time schedule, as has been the tradition for years. The young woman who has to cope with the demands of marriage and raising a family may want to drop out of training toward the end of her pregnancy, or, alternately, seek a flexible residency, in which the traditional minimal time for finishing training is waived, and an extended, less intensive program initiated. For example, two women may share one residency, and each may take twice as long to finish her formal training. Another alternative is for one individual to take one year of training in two years by working half time each year. There are other ways of arranging programs, according to the individual's and the department's particular needs.

The status of flexible training programs has been reviewed recently by Harvard's Joint Committee on the Status of Women, which issued a pamphlet listing the official flexible residencies now available.[39] The flexible residency program obviously appeals to some men as well as to young mothers: as of September 1974, seventy-six women and forty-two men were enrolled in part-time residencies; the largest number of women (43 percent) were in psychiatry (Table 14).

Table 14. Residencies in Which Women and Men
Held Part-Time Appointments
(As of 1 September 1974)

| Specialty | Number in Part-Time Residencies | | | |
	Women	Percent	Men	Percent
Anesthesiology	4	5	6	14
Child psychiatry	7	9	8	19
Family practice	1	1	3	7
General surgery	1	1	1	2
Internal medicine	6	8	1	2
Obstetrics and gynecology	2	3	—	—
Orthopedic surgery	—	—	1	2
Pathology	8	10	3	7
Pediatrics	11	14	2	5
Physical medicine and rehabilitation	1	1	—	—
Plastic surgery	—	—	1	2
Psychiatry	33	43	16	38
Radiology	2	3	—	—
Total	76	98	42	98

SOURCE: "Medical Education in the United States 1974–1975," *Journal of the American Medical Association 75th Annual Report* 234, no. 13 (29 December 1975): Table 18, 1366. Copyright 1975, American Medical Association.

Individuals can arrange for part-time residencies within a given department, even if this option is not listed in official publications. A woman expecting her first baby wrote to her faculty members in family practice. Her program, as outlined in the following letter, was unanimously approved.

---

23 March 1976

Dear Faculty Members:

I hereby request a two-month leave of absence dating from the birth of our first baby (expected in October, 1976).

I further request appointment as a half-time third-year resident for a period of two years, starting July 1, 1976.

Based on present policies and practices, I submit the following definitions of "half-time."

Clinic time: Four half-days a week

Elective time: Five half-days a week

In order to preserve maximum continuity of patient care, I plan to take all of my Clinic months contiguously, starting in July, 1976. I shall finish up with all my electives in a row. I suggest that I be included in the Clinic on-call schedule *full time* during 1976–77 (except for the two month leave of absence), and during an additional two months of 1977–78, and that I be exempt from Clinic call during the remainder of my "fourth" year.

To work a total of six months during 1976–77, I shall work full time during July and August.

July	1
August	1
September	$^1/_2$
October	0
November	0
December	$^1/_2$
January	$^1/_2$
February	$^1/_2$
March	$^1/_2$
April	$^1/_2$
May	$^1/_2$
June	$^1/_2$
Total	6

I request to be paid monthly an amount exactly half the going salary for a third-year resident for that year. I expect the full amount of vacation days, conference days, and site visit days per year to be allowed *each year* (since each day is a half-salaried day for me).

Thank you for your consideration.

Very truly yours,

There are of course specialties where training and clinical demands make a part-time residency unfeasible. Even though it has not been done traditionally, there may be ways to design part-time programs in specialties such as surgery and obstetrics and gynecology. More women must take the initiative and suggest the efficacy of such programs to doubting chairmen. Their male colleagues may also benefit from such an arrangement.

Again, as in the area of specialty training, the growing number of women seeking training will gradually result in the availability of more flexible residencies.

House-Officership and Marriage

Marriages are placed under great stress during the house-officership period, particularly during internship. In the marriage of a woman physician and a nonphysician, problems arise if the husband does not understand the pressures on his spouse. Some believe that such a mixed marriage has an advantage over the marriage of two physicians, because the nonphysician may bring another point of view to his or her spouse's world. The disadvantage of a marriage of two physicians is that during the house officer period, particularly, hours may not coincide and the couple may see little of one another. The distinct advantage is an understanding by both of the stresses the house-officership imposes.

The female house officer may be under more direct pressure than her female faculty counterpart with regard to childbearing, childrearing, and child care. For the woman who started medical school at the age of twenty-two, graduating at twenty-six, the period of house-officership coincides with her prime childbearing years. To have children and to pursue a full-time internship or residency simultaneously may be too much for some women. On the other hand, if a woman delays having children until she is in her thirties, the potential risks of pregnancy are higher.

There are no immediate solutions to the conflict between exhausting training programs and the carrying out of family responsibilities. This is an area that raises many questions for young women who seek to find out how other women doctors have managed both important duties.

Child Care

Care of her children may be a major problem for the young female physician. A reliable child-care center is often not easy to locate and, when identified, is often expensive. A woman being paid a house officer's salary may spend a great deal of it for child care. She may have to take her child to a child-care facility or to the home of a baby sitter before 7:00 A.M, when her day starts at the hospital. The long hours of training may leave the mother physically exhausted, and she may feel limited in what she can do for her child when it is returned to her in the early evening. An understanding, cooperative mate is essential if the young woman is to feel adequate in her dual roles as physician-in-training and mother.

Other Issues

One of the gravest concerns to emerge from this study focuses on women in house officer status. House-officership is a transitional position: the demands of physician training and motherhood peak simultaneously. Specialties not accustomed to flexible training programs may be challenged to change in the very near future to accommodate the growing numbers of women who enter them.

Women soon to enter house-officerships experience a more

supportive milieu in medical school than their female predecessors. The means of coping with adversity employed by women who were in the minority in medical school for years may not be necessary as more women populate medical school classes.

The specialties that, traditionally, few women entered for training may still maintain chauvinistic approaches that may take longer to change. It may be difficult for the young women who pioneer in these nontraditional specialties to cope with the negative attitudes of their male pears. They will need support and counsel from female and male colleagues in their educational quests. The dropout rates of women in residencies in surgery and obstetrics and gynecology should be carefully monitored and evaluated.

Recommendations

As we look ahead to the future of women in medicine, several questions should be raised and studied scientifically:

1. If discrimination exists, what form does it take? Many accounts are anecdotal and not quantifiable.

2. What characteristics are women students seeking in role models?

3. What constitute ideal advising and counseling services for women students, house officers, and faculty?

4. What is the best way for an individual woman to handle inequities in salary and academic standing when they arise?

5. During the childbearing and childrearing years how can academic expectations for women be altered and their promotion-tenure ladder modified?

6. What will the training experience be like for women who enter specialties such as surgery that have been nontraditional fields for most women?

7. Will women enter academia in greater numbers?

8. Will qualified women attain administrative positions in the medical centers in the future?

9. As women become accepted in their new roles what will be the incidence of illnesses such as ulcers and hypertension, and of suicide?

Summary

The major purpose of this study was to begin to evaluate developments that have taken place over the last decade in a sample of the nation's medical colleges, secondary to the increasing number of women students. The data are based on the overall impressions of the individuals interviewed.

Change takes time. Despite this fact, many differences were noted in comparing the medical centers of the mid-1960s to those of the mid-1970s. Whether these occurred secondary to the expansion in the enrollment of women, to federal legislation, to private philanthropic support, to societal pressure, or to a combination of all factors, is debatable.

Today's woman applicant faces a more welcoming attitude at the medical school than did her counterpart a decade ago. She may even be interviewed by a female faculty member or senior student who understands some of the concerns unique to the female candidate. Her application receives the same consideration as that of male applicants. Once in medical school she finds many other women in her class. Her male peers may be aware and supportive of the issues that concern women. Female and male faculty undoubtedly have a greater awareness of the female presence in their classes.

A woman faces problems in her day-to-day existence in medical school: not all her male friends think she should be there, nor do all female and male faculty members support her presence enthusiastically. As she looks for female role models among faculty and deans, she finds few. Her experience may be marked by inconsistency — positive support by some colleagues and mentors; a neutral stance by some; subtle discrimination by others; and overt hostility by still others. She has to clarify her professional and personal identity as a woman physician in this milieu. In general, however, she feels supported; if she doesn't, she can seek counseling from within the medical school.

The woman in clinical training begins to look to female house staff for role models. She finds a greater variety of specialty choices among these young women than among the few female faculty members. She may find that fellow house officers understand her aspirations and interests better than her female teachers, because the former went through adolescence during similar times of societal change. She may be particularly impressed by a woman house officer in a nontraditional specialty such as surgery. The issues of combining marriage, children, and a profession are bound to surface for the woman who is newly married or planning to marry. For the woman who has children, these issues may take other forms, such as finding adequate child-care facilities.

As a young woman in 1976 approaches her house-officership she sees accessibility to virtually every training program. In fact some specialties that were unenthusiastic about women ten years ago actively seek her application. She is concerned about combining a career and a family, and seeks female role models who have accomplished this successfully. She finds a limited number of flexible training programs and a shortage of day-care centers at the university medical centers.

The woman on the medical faculty in 1976 continues to find few other women serving in similar positions, and very few in the deans' offices. She is impressed by the number of young female medical students and house officers, and she may be supportive, neutral, or unsupportive of her young female colleagues.

The woman faculty member knows her salary and those of her female colleagues are more equitable than in the 1960s. Chairmen of departments are more aware of her presence on the faculty compared to a decade ago. The chairman may in fact be *too* aware of her presence and assign her to too many committees to meet medical school demands placed on him/her. Individual women may be actively recruited by other medical centers to fill their affirmative action requirements.

Women in medicine may clarify a need to join together and form action-oriented groups that are mutually supportive and available to young female colleagues.

In general there have been many positive changes in the status of women physicians, house officers, and students in the medical centers. New problems, such as stresses women undergo in training programs not accustomed to having women, must be anticipated, and prevented from occurring. If prevention is not possible, early recognition is vital.

The future for women in medicine in the United States over the next several decades is bright.

Conclusions

The major findings in this study that reflect positive changes for women physicians and students in medical school, comparing the mid-1960s to the mid-1970s, are as follows:

1. Nearly four times as many women students were enrolled in the nation's medical schools in 1974–75 than in 1964–65, and nearly five times as many in 1975–76 than in 1965–66.

2. There is an increase in the number of women at the house staff level, reflecting the increment of women at the medical student level.

3. Admissions committees in those medical centers visited are uniformly interested in admitting the best students, regardless of sex.

4. Women faculty serve on most admissions committees; in several schools, women students are also members of admissions committees. Such participation sensitizes male members to issues of particular concern to female candidates.

5. Female students corroborate equity in admissions procedures. Most had experienced good interviews; for those who did not, the consensus is that this frequently represented an individual interviewer's bias against women rather than a school's attitude.

6. Male students in general are supportive of their female colleagues, and even defend them when a professor makes a remark that is offensive to the females in the class.

7. Female students have more classmates of their own sex with whom to associate, and thus more variety. Some feel that in the current milieu association with female colleagues is no longer a necessity; others seek a closeness with other women in their class and usually find it.

8. Faculty in general, male and female, are supportive and

are motivated to educate female students; some women students report this is not uniformly true.

9. Female house staff and senior medical students are increasingly serving as role models for young female medical students.

10. Supportive services, such as group counseling for women, are being developed in some settings. These services are new, however, and are the exception rather than the rule.

11. In most of the institutions visited, counseling services for students with academic or personal problems are equally accessible to all. The problems encountered in these services are frequently the same for women and men.

12. Salaries, promotions, and tenure are gradually becoming more equitable for women faculty.

13. A dean for women is not a necessity, as the goal is to integrate women into the medical schools; the concept of a dean for women might therefore be inimicable to this goal.

14. Women faculty are freer to move from a medical center that is unsupportive of their professional growth than their counterparts were in the 1960s. This is true even if the move results in the disruption of their husbands' careers and their children's education.

15. An increasing number of women graduates are seeking and gaining entry to training programs in specialties that formerly were not widely available to them: surgery and obstetrics and gynecology, for example.

16. In general, male and female faculty and students are optimistic about the future of women in medicine.

17. The many developments cited are most likely the combined effects of a changing society, government support of equal rights for women, and private philanthropic contributions.

*   *   *   *

The major findings that suggest a lack of change or a loss of previous positive gains are as follows:

1. Some female students believe there is still evidence of discrimination against them by individual faculty and colleagues.

2. There are few flexible medical school programs that accommodate an individual's unique needs.

3. The ratio of women doctors on academic faculties has decreased by approximately 5 percent in the last decade.

4. There is a dearth of excellent faculty female role models for female students.

5. Few faculty women hold administrative offices in the nation's medical schools.

6. Pediatrics, anesthesiology, physical medicine, and public health and preventive medicine are the specialties most women are encouraged to enter, reflecting training patterns of ten years ago.

7. The successful combination of professional (student, trainee, or faculty) and family responsibilities still presents problems.

8. Day-care centers are not usually available at university medical centers; outside child-care arrangements are expensive.

9. Faculty women are being asked to serve on many committees, and thus, as opposed to the phenomenon of the 1960s when they were "undercommitteed," they are uniformly "overcommitteed." The few women on the medical faculties want to respond and participate, but may feel guilty if they have to refuse.

10. Older faculty women who have attained status in the medical milieu, which was unwelcoming to women in the past, may be unsupportive and hypercritical of the accomplishments of their younger female colleagues.

11. Women in transition, such as young female house officers in a predominantly male training program, may be at particularly high risk for academic or emotional problems, as there is no precedent for their presence on those services.

12. There is a dearth of literature on the difficulties women face in the medical milieu of the mid-1970s. As old problems are solved, new ones must be identified. In the interest of preventive medicine, problems should be anticipated and, through intervention, prevented from arising.

13. As in other areas of life, change for women in medical education is coming about slowly.

Acknowledgments

I would like to extend my gratitude to John Z. Bowers, M.D., president of the Josiah Macy, Jr. Foundation, for affording me the opportunity to do this study; to Mary I. Bunting, Ph.D., for her consultation; to Mrs. Carleen Wilenius, Ms. Maxine Bleich, Miss Harriet Purdy, and Mrs. Betty Satterwhite for their assistance; and to the many helpful individuals in the medical schools I visited who were most gracious and welcoming, and who gave unselfishly of their time. I would like also to thank the students, house staff, and faculty of the University of Rochester for their interest and support, particularly Gilbert Forbes, M.D., Robert Hoekelman, M.D., Ruth Lawrence, M.D., John Romano, M.D., and Olle Jane Sahler, M.D.

Notes*

1. R. Baker, *The First Woman Doctor — The Story of Elizabeth Blackwell, M.D.*
2. R. Truax, *The Doctors Jacobi.*
3. Esther Pohl Lovejoy, *Women Doctors of the World.*
4. Carol Lopate, *Women in Medicine.*
5. John Romano, "More Point than Counterpoint."
6. Quoted in Lovejoy, *Women Doctors* (see note 3).
7. "Undergraduate Medical Education," 1340.
8. Ibid., 1341.
9. Davis G. Johnson and Edwin B. Hutchins, "Doctor or Dropout," 1140.
10. "Undergraduate Medical Education," 1138.
11. Harvard University Joint Committee, "Annual Report, 1974–75."
12. Davis G. Johnson, "The Medical Student, 1975," 37–53.
13. *Medical School Admission Requirements 1977–78.*
14. Lopate, *Women in Medicine* (see note 4).

---

* Notes for these chapters are abbreviated. Complete references may be found in the Bibliography, beginning on p. 105.

15. H. Paul Jolly and Thomas A. Larson, *Participation of Women and Minorities in U.S. Medical School Faculties.*
16. Harvard University Joint Committee, "Report of the Student Task Force."
17. Mary C. Howell and D. Hiatt, "Do Women Student Health Services Discriminate Against Women," 359.
18. Elaine Hilberman, et al., "Support Groups for Women in Medical School," 867.
19. Harvard University Joint Committee, "Obstacles to Equal Education at Harvard Resulting from Discrimination."
20. A. E. Bayer and H. S. Astin, "Sex Differentials in the Academic Reward System," 796.
21. Lopate, *Women in Medicine* (see note 4).
22. Jolly and Larson, *Participation of Women* (see note 15).
23. M. H. Witte, A. J. Arem, and M. Holguin, "Women Physicians in United States Medical Schools," 211.
24. Bayer and Astin, "Sex Differentials" (see note 20).
25. E. W. Hart and P. W. Diridoni, "Status of Staff Women and Minorities at the University of California at San Francisco."
26. "Discrimination Widespread: Being Female Still a Handicap to M.D.'s," 1.
27. Elizabeth Drouilhet, "The Fifty Years of Vassar I Have Seen."
28. "A Married Doctress," 187.
29. Nancy Roeske, "Women in Medicine—A New Epoch."
30. E. M. Short, "Women in the AFCR," 123.
31. "Special Report of the Medical Education and Research Committee of the American Medical Women's Association," 27.
32. P. Q. Hall, S. M. Malcolm, and S. E. Posner, "Conference on Minority Women Scientists," 457.
33. "Graduate Medical Education," 1362.
34. "Special Studies in Graduate Medical Education," 1553.
35. Ibid.
36. "Special Studies in Graduate Medical Education," 1250.
37. "Graduate Medical Education," 1365.
38. E. McGrath and C. N. Zimet, "Female and Male Medical Students."
39. Harvard University Joint Committee, "Institutions Offering Reduced-Schedule Training."

Appendix 1

This form was completed by medical students and house officers interviewed in the course of the study.

Interview # _____

Date _____

STUDY OF WOMEN AND MEDICAL SCHOOLS

NAME _____ AGE _____ SEX _____

CURRENT INSTITUTION _____

CHECK AS APPROPRIATE:

Medical Student	*House Officer*
_____ 1st yr.	_____ intern
_____ 2nd yr.	_____ 1st yr. res.
_____ 3rd yr.	_____ 2nd yr. res.
_____ 4th yr.	_____ 3rd yr. res.
	_____ other

PLEASE COMPLETE APPLICABLE PORTIONS OF THE FOLLOWING:

Undergraduate School _____ Year _____

Medical School _____ Year _____

Postgraduate Training _____ Year _____

_____ Year _____

Current Department(s) _____

Marital Status: _____ Married _____ Single _____ Other

Number of Children _____ Ages: _____, _____, _____, _____, _____

PLEASE ANSWER THE FOLLOWING QUESTIONS (Rank each item – 1, low; 5, high):
1. Why did you choose medicine as a career? (Rank each item according to its importance in your decision: 1, no importance; 5, most importance.)

	1	2	3	4	5
Interest in biological sciences					
Known role models					
Desire to work with people					
Secure career					
Financial attraction					
Family's encouragement					
Other (describe)					

When did you decide on medicine as a career? _____ pre-high school _____ high school _____ undergraduate school _____ other (describe)

2. How did you choose your specialty? (Rank each item according to its importance in your decision: 1, no importance; 5, most importance.)

	1	2	3	4	5
Known role models					
Like working with people					
Family encouragement					
Financial attraction					
Anticipated acceptance in field (i.e. inaccessibility of some fields to women)					
Other (describe)					

3. From whom do you receive your emotional support? (Rank each choice according to its significance for you: 1, no support; 5, most support.)

	1	2	3	4	5
Peers					
Spouse					
Parents					
Superiors					
Other (specify)					

Appendix 2

The following forms (Appendixes 2 a, b, c, d, e, and f) were utilized for individual interviews during the site visits in order to obtain uniform data.

Appendix 2a

ADMISSIONS COMMITTEE

Individual _____

Position _____

University _____

Date _____

Explain Study (comments).
1. Number of applicants over several years.
   Male vs. female (any written data)?
2. Admissions procedures.
   What is the process? Any differences, male vs. female?
   a. How interviewers chosen for individual applicant.
   b. Committee on Admissions—male/female representation? Student representation?
   c. Choice of men different from women?—Comparative data of MCAT scores, college averages available?
      General feeling about married women—married men; older women—older men; older married women—older married men.
3. Applicants—changes in women applicants; men applicants.
   a. Quality—1950 to now.
   b. Motivation—1950 to now.
   c. Idealism—1950 to now.
   d. Why students choose medicine?
4. Financial aid, men vs. women?
5. Quota for minorities (racial) or women?
6. Comment on medical school admissions at present versus 1950s and 1960s—particularly in regard to women. Particularly probing for changes observed secondary to increased number of women in schools?
7. Critical mass phenomena.
8. Other contacts.

Appendix 2b

DEAN'S OFFICE

Individual _____

Position _____

University _____

Date _____

Explain Study (comments).
1. Request catalogue.
2. Observed changes in medical schools secondary to increased numbers of women.
   a. Before World War II – any female students?
   b. Data on number of women medical students and women faculty over time.
   c. Data on *current* number of women medical students by class, and number of women faculty.
3. Advisor system – any different men vs. women?
   Women's dean? Should there be?
4. Problems – male medical students/faculty:
   a. Academic?
   b. Personal?
5. Reasons male and female students drop out of school.
6. Career choice of students, male vs. female? Changes over time?
7. Reverse discrimination now?
8. Critical mass phenomena.
9. Ground rules of visit.

Appendix 2c

REGISTRAR

Individual _____

Position _____

University _____

Date _____

Explain study.
1. Comments in general.
2. Academic problems – men vs. women – 1950s vs. 1970s.
   Describe specific problems, if more present in women than men.
3. Drop-outs by class – why for men/why for women?
   (Academic, financial, personal – exactly why?) Any written data?

4. How does decision to drop out get made?
   If student decides to drop out, what efforts are made to work with him/her? Male vs. female?
5. Quality of students — 1950s vs. 1970s — women vs. men.
   a. Quality — grade point averages.
   b. Motivation.
   c. Idealism.
6. From his/her perspective, what are changes secondary to increasing number of women in the medical schools?
7. Other contacts.

Appendix 2d

FACULTY

Name _____

Date _____

School _____

1. Explain Study.
2. Any other specialty would have liked to enter?
   If yes, what?
   Related to sex?
3. Number of women on department faculty?
   Number of men on department faculty?
   Change in last ten years?
4. Advise house staff? Men vs. women. Medical students? Men vs. women.
   Advise men different than women?
5. Married, particular problems?
   Occupation spouse?
   Support by spouse? Encouragement? Household tasks?
6. Children? Particular problems?
   Day care available?
   How handle child care?
7. Single, particular problems (poorer remuneration, isolation, dating, loneliness)?
8. Flexible schedule?
9. Discrimination in:
   a. Salary?
   b. Tenure?
   c. Promotion?
   d. Space/secretarial help?
   e. Flexible hours?
   f. Mobility?
   g. Other?
   Other discriminatory things: unconscious slights, off committees, sexist behavior, exploitation, harrassment?
10. Professional goals next five years?
11. Comments on the effect of increasing numbers of women in medical schools.
12. Additional contacts.

Appendix 2e

HOUSE STAFF

Name _____

Date _____

School _____

Explain Study.
1. Fill out identifying information and grids.
2. Internship admissions interviews (here)?
   a. Negative comments re women in your specialty?
      Very frequent___Frequent___Infrequent___
   b. Questions asked not asked of opposite sex?
      Very frequent___Frequent___Infrequent___
   c. Is there a specialty you would have entered if you were not a female? Yes___
      No___If yes, what?
3. Number of women in your training program?
   Number of men in your training program?
4. Role models in your specialty? Men? Women?
   a. Availability?
   b. Accessibility?
   c. What do you look for in role models?
5. Advisor system?
   How advisor/advisee teamed?
   Special advisors for men in your department?
6. Peers
   Like sex – Very good friends___Good friends___Not good friends___
   Opposite sex – Very good friends___Good friends___Not good friends___
   Specific problems?
7. Evidence of discrimination against you?
   Very frequent___Frequent___Infrequent___
   Explain:
8. Leisure facilities (men vs. women; availability; accessiblity)?
9. On-call facilities (men vs. women)?
10. Dressing rooms – surgery – women with nurses?
11. Married? Occupation spouse?
    Support from spouse – encouragement, household tasks, etc.
    Children? Particular problems? Day care available?
12. Flexible training program for married women – any provisions for flexibility?
13. Single, particular problems (isolation, dating, loneliness)?
14. On-call schedule – same men vs. women?
15. Ten-year professional goals?
16. What do you think of women in medicine?
    What do you think of men in medicine?
17. Effects of increasing number of women in medicine?
18. Additional contacts.

Appendix 2f

MEDICAL STUDENTS

Name _____

School _____

Date _____

Explain Study.
1. Fill out identifying information and grids.
2. Admissions interviews (here)?
    a. Negative comments about women in medicine?
       Very frequent___Frequent___Infrequent___
    b. Questions asked you not asked of opposite sex?
       Very frequent___Frequent___Infrequent___
       Explain:
3. Role models—Men? Women?
    a. Availability?
    b. Accessibility?
    c. What do you look for in role models?
4. Advisor system?
    a. How advisor/advisee teamed?
    b. Differences, men vs. women students?
    c. Special advisors for women?
5. If you had problems, to whom would you go?
    a. Academic?
    b. Personal?
    c. Equal accessibility, women and men students?
6. Peers:
    a. Same sex—Very good friends___Good friends___Not good friends___
    b. Opposite sex—Very good friends___Good friends___Not good friends___
    c. Specific problems
7. Evidence of discrimination against you?
    Very Frequent___Frequent___Infrequent___Never___
    Explain:
8. Facilities provided for leisure time (women vs. men; availability; accessibility)?
9. On-call facilities (men vs. women) describe.
10. If married, particular problems? Single, problems?
11. If children, particular problems? Different men vs. women?

Summary of the Conference

John Walsh

Ten years ago less than 8 percent of physicians in training and practice in the United States were women, and most discussions of women in medicine dwelled inevitably on their minority status. The social climate of the 1960s was hostile to such inequality, however, and recent years have brought a major increase in the number of women enrolled in American medical schools.*

One purpose of this conference on Women in Medicine was to assess the progress of women physicians in the past decade; while the surge in the representation of women in medical education was welcomed as the dominant development in that period, it was not interpreted as proof that the problems they encounter have been resolved. The locus of concern has shifted from the issue of the numbers of women students in medical school to the question of their experiences in the next phase of training — the residency. The consensus of the conference was that professional and personal pressures bear most heavily on women physicians when they serve as house officers in hospitals, and that it is during this stage of training that changes are most urgently needed.

This does not imply that the problems women encounter as undergraduate medical students or as practicing physicians have disappeared: they can in fact be expressed in very much the same terms as those in which they were formulated ten or even twenty years ago. Elizabeth McAnarney's report provided a starting point for the conference and a statement of the current status of women in medicine.

---

* In 1975–76 women represented 16 percent of the graduates, 21 percent of the intermediate students, and 24 percent of the first-year students, compared with 1964–65 when only 7.7 percent of all students enrolled were female.

A majority of the Macy conference participants were mature women physicians who have made successful careers in academic medicine. Most of them have done research relevant to the theme of the conference or have had direct experience with efforts to ameliorate the difficulties of women physicians. Their viewpoint, therefore, was generally that of persons who have known discrimination themselves; who are sensitive to the predicament of those who one conferee called "our professional daughters"; and who have not only survived the rigors of the system but are enjoying careers of substantial achievement.

The discussion concentrated primarily on women physicians, not on women in other jobs in the health field; academic medicine, not private practice, was the main focus of the conference. The atmosphere was informal and the style discursive; no rigorous attempt was made to make recommendations or to set priorities in detail. There was, however, a considerable measure of agreement both on the analyses of problems and on the actions desirable. This summary concentrates on the main points of agreement, particularly in relation to residency training.

In a sense, the conference evolved into an examination of women in graduate medical education and of the special difficulties they face if they seek to combine residency training with the bearing and rearing of children. As the discussion developed it acquired the broader dimensions of a critique of graduate medical education itself, and revealed a consensus that the future role of women in medicine is not simply to take their place as equals to men but to change the system itself.

Residency

For the physician, the residency marks the passage from student status to full professional standing. During this period — two to five years depending on the specialty — physicians undergo the formative experience that largely determines the course their careers will take. That experience is gained by working extremely long hours, often under conditions of maximum stress. Medical residencies differ from other kinds of professional training in the obvious respect that a resident's actions often have a decisive effect on a patient's health or even her or his life. But, as Leah M. Lowenstein of Boston University School of Medicine pointed out, the medical residency is also unusual in graduate education because it is characterized by a "time commitment rather than a learning commitment." She quoted John Millis to the effect that these years are marked by less organization, more divided responsibility, and fewer standards than other stages of medical training,[1] and that, in addition to learning in the hospital and teaching medical students and other residents, house officers are often obliged to perform various menial tasks.

The rigors of the residency were summed up at the conference in the phrase "the hundred-hour week." Whether an exaggeration of present reality, as some conferees argued, or, as others insisted, still a fact of life for residents, the hundred-hour work week retains its power as a symbol. There was certainly little disagreement that the residency remains an endurance test. As Lowenstein described it:

> Interns often suffer from sleep deprivation . . . perform as automatons, are laggard in their thinking, develop unreal, callous attitudes toward their patients, and make errors. The immense number of on-call hours are not consumed with learning alone: [but in some settings with] wheeling patients to X-ray, running to labs with blood specimens, and generally performing services not usually necessary for learning to become a good doctor.

All of this applies to men as well as to women, of course, but the years of residency—normally served when a doctor is between the ages of twenty-six and thirty—are regarded as a woman's optimal childbearing years. Women physicians are acutely aware that the risks of childbearing for both baby and mother progressively increase after a woman passes thirty. The pressures on married women physicians are therefore often greatest precisely at the time when the professional demands on them are least manageable.

In the past many women doctors have been willing to assume the "superwoman" role by accepting the double burden of full responsibility for a medical career and marriage and motherhood. Now, however, the "quality-of-life" demands from younger women and men in the profession are resulting in significantly altered attitudes toward the medical work ethic.

Discrimination

The conferees agreed that women house officers face more than vestigial forms of discrimination, both institutional and individual. In many hospitals unequal or unsuitable dressing facilities and overnight sleeping accomodations for women persist, for example, and they continue to encounter baldly or blandly sexist "why-aren't-you-at-home-having-babies" attitudes from faculty. Most damaging at every stage of the residency is the assumption on the part of many male physicians that women are less reliable than men because of divided loyalties or because of the presumption that the woman will sooner or later drop out of training or practice.

Current pressures appear to be greatest on women pioneering in specialties that traditionally have been male preserves— obstetrics and gynecology, urology, and surgery. In these specialties, particularly, the conditions for women residents compare unfavorably with those for women medical students. Not only has the increased enrollment of women in medical schools provided strength in numbers, but the women's movement has given them a sense of unity and, in many cases, the organization and techniques to act effectively against discriminatory policies and sexist attitudes. In addition, shifts in general social attitudes seem to have resulted in much stronger support for women medical students from men students and sympathetic male faculty.

As residents, on the other hand, women tend to be isolated. The attitudes of male residents toward women peers is said to be more negative, again particularly in specialties that have been male enclaves or where the competitive "pyramid system" of advancement survives. Male residents often band together in mutual support groups from which women often seem to be excluded, thus heightening their isolation. Not surprisingly, the conduct of male residents is frequently believed to reflect the attitudes of the faculty members in charge. Ironically, women residents may be the victims of "gender typing" by members of their own sex, since nurses and other women in hospital jobs may harbor ambivalent feelings about women physicians and treat them accordingly.

Much of the discrimination encountered by women house officers can be classed as covert rather than overt, reflecting the difficulties of male-female relationships in society at large. Although examples are hard to document, cumulatively they are considered very important. The basic predicament of women was expressed by Elva O. Poznansky of the University of Michigan:

> Another problem for academic women is sheer loneliness. Generally women are recognizing this and finding each other, but the casual friendliness that men find in a new institution rarely includes a woman. In fact when a male academician does make a friendship with a woman it is labeled and underscored primarily because it demands a special effort. Perhaps this is natural, in that such friendships scrape the border between friendliness and sexuality and are more clearly defined and tabooed than in male-to-male relationships. These subtle differences are shown in the way women physicians in academia are usually referred to as Dr. so-and-so long after their male peers are addressed by their first names. It is as if the male academicians need to keep up an artificial wall with their female peers [though not] with their male peers.

This uneasiness poses special problems for women residents in establishing relationships with "mentors," a connection recognized as a practical necessity for residents with ambitions in academic medicine. Informal access is regarded as essential to the mentor-protegé bond, and it is much more difficult, for example, for a woman resident to play squash or to go to dinner with a male faculty member than it is for a male resident. Yet it is conceded to be equally necessary for a woman resident to do a rotation with a professor with prestige — the odds are great that this person will be male — and get a good recommendation. Women therefore tend to be handicapped in forming the required relationships that are normally cultivated through a good deal of unselfconscious, informal contact.

Women resent these persisting patterns of prejudice. Several conferees, however, alluded to expectations that changes in social attitudes, already evident in undergraduate medical education, will favorably affect residency training, particularly as the numbers of women increase in all specialties.

Obstacles to Change

Although a strong feeling exists that flexible residencies present a practical alternative to the marathon schedule of the traditional residency, two major factors operate in favor of the present modes of organization and scheduling.

First, the financing of residencies presents unique problems. In a resident's training, service and education are almost inextricably mixed. Third-party payers for medical care, including the federal government, are insistent that they not subsidize education through payment for patient care. Efforts to control the costs of hospital care are certain to increase in the future, and any changes in residency programs that appear to raise costs will almost certainly be resisted.

The second major obstacle is the view that a total immersion experience is necessry for the training of competent physicians. This traditionalist view, which is probably held by a majority of those who make policy on residencies, was cogently expressed during the concluding session of the conference by J. Robert Willson, who, as chairman of the Department of Obstetrics and Gynecology at the University of Michigan Medical School, represents one of the specialties into which women are only beginning to move in significant numbers:

> I have heard much about the problems of being a woman student or house officer, and how difficult it is to combine careers during this phase of professional development. I have heard little, however, about the quality of the educational experience. Shorter hours, fewer nights on call, more time at home are all fine and desirable, but they can't be made available within the present time frame of most residency programs without compro-

mising the quality of the experience. It takes a certain amount of time to acquire information, develop the skills, and to learn to apply them to the practice of a medical or surgical specialty. I could reduce the work week of my house officers to forty hours, but only if there were half again as many and only if they remained in the program for six rather than four years. I have no interest in training incompetent obstetrician-gynecologists, and you have no interest in programs that prepare women inadequately.

I have heard you say that women are "afraid of success" and that they are unwilling to make the commitments necessary to obtain high-level positions in medicine. You are not very good examples of this, because you all quite obviously have done what was necessary to get where you are. What you may be overlooking is that most men are not willing to make this commitment either, but that those who are have had little competition from women because there have been so few to compete. This will change inevitably as more women are graduated and are prepared to compete for these presumably prestigious positions.

You can't change it from the inside while there are so few of you. If I may be so bold as to make a suggestion, it seems to me that you should be concentrating on the young women now in medical schools and in residencies, convincing them that the best way to prove themselves is to be able to compete for residencies and faculty positions equally with their male peers. You certainly could make full use of the affirmative action programs in your universities to help capable women obtain positiions in residencies. You'll not make much progress by saying, "It's unfair we aren't already there," or by telling departmental chairmen they are unfit to develop an educational program or to provide medical care for women because they are men and don't understand the problems. You will be able to achieve the necessary advances by continuing to prove in increasing numbers that women are equally as competent as men in any branch of medicine they may choose to enter.

Flexible Residencies

Flexible residencies appeared to the conferees to be the most promising mitigator of the hundred-hour work week. This alternative is not a theoretical one: flexible residencies are already operating, most of them in primary specialties, in at least two hundred institutions with some five hundred programs. The challenge is to obtain information about existing programs, to make it widely available, and to encourage the propagation of the flexible-residency option.

Information Dissemination

The information gap seems to be in the process of being closed. The Joint Committee on the Status of Women at Harvard, the group that seems to have done most in the cause of what it terms reduced-schedule residencies, assembled a partial list of two hundred institutions with such residencies. The committee published an unverified list late in 1975, and, in the spring of 1976, a verified list with a somewhat reduced number of institutions and programs. The group now has money from the Rockefeller Family Fund to carry out a survey in order to expand the listing to include all institutions with reduced-schedule programs.

There seems little doubt about whether or not there is interest in such information. An article by a member of the staff of the Joint Committee contained a single line asking if anyone were interested in flexible residencies: in ten days she got five hundred replies. The committee now plans to initiate a program under which medical students might provide information about the sort of residencies they wish to share. The committee would act as a clearinghouse, at least temporarily, with Shirley Driscoll of the Boston Hospital for Women overseeing the program for a year. It was suggested that the National Internship and Residency Matching Program might subsequently adopt such a project.

Individual Programs

Some flexible residencies have been the result of individual initiative. Jan Soulé, who recently completed a residency in pediatrics at the University of California at San Diego, told how she had negotiated a reduced-schedule residency. The departmental chairman's openness to the idea was the key to its acceptance. (Soulé noted that one of her points in support of a flexible schedule was a reference to the chairman's inviolable daily tennis commitment.) Her proposal was that she and a "partner" would receive credit and pay for half-time training while, in fact, each worked two-thirds to three-quarters time. There can be unforeseen personal hitches as well as administrative problems in these arrangements, as Soulé's own experience illustrated: when her partner dropped out of the arrangement, Soulé resumed a full-time schedule. The shared residency had worked well enough, however, for the department to be receptive to such plans in the future.

Long-term Programs

In addition to arrangements made by enterprising individuals, there are also some well-established, long-term programs of reduced-schedule residencies. At New York Medical College, for example, over a period of seven years forty-four women have been involved in part-time psychiatric residencies and thirty-four women and thirteen men in residencies in other specialties. It is interesting and probably not too surprising that psychiatry, which deals with personal relationships and stress, should be concerned about the pressures on its own residents.

The Radcliffe Study

A pioneer effort to encourage women to undertake flexible residencies was begun in the mid-1960s by the Radcliffe Institute with the financial support of the Macy Foundation. Between 1966 and the early 1970s some seventy-six grants totalling $160,000 were made through a special program for women physicians. While the recipients ranged from medical students to senior residents, a substantial number were continuing or resuming medical careers by serving half-time residencies in the Boston area. The program directors recognized that many women with children encounter financial difficulties in completing professional training. At a time when interns' and residents' salaries were relatively much lower than they are now, the grants provided funds for child care and other necessary expenses, in many cases making it possible for the recipients to follow medical careers. The grants were made under the institute's Program of Independent Study, which was designed in part to prepare women to move into posts of greater responsibility. Because of current concern about a dearth of women in leadership roles in medicine, the experience of the women who received fellowships under the Radcliffe program is, potentially, of considerable interest. No detailed final evaluation of the program has yet been made, but the conferees agreed that a retrospective study would be valuable.

Evaluation

A major obstacle to the wider adoption of flexible residencies is the failure to evaluate the effectiveness of residency programs. One source of solid information is expected to be a follow-up study of a part-time, primary-care residency program at the Medical College of Pennsylvania funded by the federal government.

Government Action

Several conferees suggested that the greatest impetus for change in graduate medical education in the immediate future may indeed come from the federal government. In particular, a section of the health manpower training bill before the Congress at the time of the conference, and which survived in the version of the bill enacted into law, should have real impact. It requires that teaching hospitals and medical schools that receive government funds shall establish reduced-schedule residencies in primary care specialties. Under the provision, two people would share one residency post, each working two-thirds or three-quarters of the training time and each receiving appropriate credit and half pay. The conferees considered these terms realistic. It is worth noting that inclusion of this section in the bill is attributed largely to the efforts of two women on Harvard's Joint Committee on the Status of Women.

One of the possible disadvantages of this sort of legislation, according to Lowenstein, is that it might channel even more women into primary care specialties, thus putting them outside the specialties that many professionals consider the mainstream of medicine. Lowenstein cited the action of one woman chairman of a department of pediatrics at a prestigious medical school in abolishing reduced-schedule residencies in her department because of apprehension that through them women might become second-class medical citizens. There is the question of whether men will be antagonized by what they may consider special privileges for women in the flexible residencies, and recurring doubts exist about whether training will be intensive enough if undergone on a part-time basis. It was agreed, however, that the main criterion to be applied to changes in the residency schedules should be not whether they are desirable for residents, male or female, but whether they are in the best interests of patients.

Conclusions

The basic case made for reform of the residency is that the changes women physicians are attempting to bring about in graduate medical education would improve conditions for doctors of both sexes, for patients, and therefore for society. The thesis put forward is that the public has expected its doctors to be superhuman. Medical education is therefore producing frustrated professionals and, as a consequence, the system is seriously flawed. This is the critique that provides the rationale for reform.

Agents of Change

A major premise was that the increase in the number of women in medical education means that they are moving toward positions of equity, if not of numerical equality, in medicine. Lloyd Elam of Meharry Medical College observed that, formerly, attitudes about women in medicine relied on the model of women as a minority. Now that the numbers of women have expanded substantially, it is appropriate to use another model, that of "women as change agents," not for the benefit of women only, but to "change the whole system so that it's better for everyone."

Nancy A. Roeske of Indiana University, on the subject of the rising numbers of women in medicine, warned against "equating numbers of women with Utopia." There has been a

> . . . prior assumption that if we increase the number of women in medicine this will have a . . . beneficial effect on the health care of women and men, and . . . improve the quality of the health care provided by women physicians and by men physicians. But we do not actually know that this is going to happen.

Roeske cautioned that "We are in a period of very rapid social evolution," and must take care not to mix "hypotheses and conclusions" — a warning that should be heeded in designing, executing, and evaluating new programs.

> We are assuming that changing the number of women in medicine will benefit the care of patients . . . that women physicians will be more receptive to the needs of women patients, and thus improve their care. In addition, the woman physician should educate male colleagues about the psychology of women. Furthermore, we are assuming that women physicians will serve as a model of self-realization for other women and men. Finally, a related assumption is that more women will seek expression because they were cared for by a woman physician . . . these are assumptions and may not necessarily become facts.

Call for Research

Few conferences conclude without a call for more research, but the Macy conferees, while honoring this tradition, were more precise than is customary in pinpointing the directions such research should take. Beatrice Levine, a social scientist and planner, provided a review of current research on women in medicine from the perspective of her work on a recent, broad-scale, exploratory study of women in health professions schools sponsored by the Department of Health, Education, and Welfare. Levine remarked that there is a substantial body of research on women in medicine that has focused primarily on the effect of the system on the individual and that has provided a basis for federal antidiscrimination actions resulting in more open access for women to medical education.

In the past much effort has been devoted to studies of trends dealing with issues at the national level. It is desirable to repeat these studies in a systematic way, since research often loses value if it is not updated — and changes today are occurring very rapidly. Such studies, however, are beyond the capability of individuals or small research groups; they should be conducted by organizations such as the American Medical Association or the Association of American Medical Colleges.

What is necessary, in addition, said Levine, is "action research," for example, on various flexible-residency programs. Also needed is institutional research on individual medical schools to investigate areas such as admissions policies, attrition, and operating styles to gain a clearer idea of what differentiates successful from unsuccessful programs.

Levine and others at the conference urged that researchers look closely at the policies of federal and state governments, as well as of medical associations and specialty boards, to determine how they affect women in medicine. Current legislative and regulatory activities also deserve close attention: some may possibly have negative implications for women.

Levine noted that cost-benefit analyses in the area of medical training and practice are particularly important, since such analyses have shown that women physicians have lower productivity than men. She argued that in these analyses it is necessary to raise such questions as: "What do you mean by cost?"; "What do you mean by benefit?" Such studies should not focus simply on a "dollars-in, dollars-out" basis. A measure of quality should be added.

Pragmatism was the pervasive attitude during the conference, especially toward research and experimental programs. Joseph Katz of the State University of New York at Stony Brook, among others, stressed the need to incorporate careful evaluation methods into the design of research and pilot programs. Conference Chairman Mary I. Bunting at the final session observed that those examining the problems of women in medicine are talking about a "frontier of ignorance," and that it is essential to learn more about how to work on such a frontier. She said it was necessary to warn the federal government about the perils of rushing into major programs "before you know what some of the by-products are and what some of the problems are." The model the government should foster, she maintained, is that of the National Science Foundation. People with valid ideas should be able to apply for government support and, if they make their cases well enough, be able to undertake projects, have them evaluated, and then reported in a way that would make their findings available to others.

Bunting also expressed the hope that the federal government will take steps to relieve the confusion that now besets the financing of residencies. Payments from federal programs are important in providing residents' salaries, but, legally, these funds cannot be used to underwrite educational activities. This conflict needs to be resolved.

Another important research target cited is the approximately 36 percent of women physicians currently in practice in the United States who are foreign medical graduates (FMGs). Today most new FMGs come from India, Korea, and the Philippines, and their problems and the effects of their educational and cultural backgrounds on their performances are not well understood.

Communication and Action

Despite the big increase in the numbers of women in medical school, there appears to be a continuing need for women's "support groups" in the medical setting. These groups, products of the feminist movement, are established to serve consciousness-raising and morale-boosting functions as well as to identify and help solve women's problems.

Committees on the status of women have been created at several medical schools. The Joint Committee at Harvard, cited as a pacemaker among such groups, apparently owes its effectiveness, at least in part, to the fact that it is a regular committee of the medical, dental, and public health schools, and has a small, paid staff whose members can give full time to committee projects.

Regarding the concerns and characteristics of women medical students, Marion K. Jacobs of the University of California at Irvine suggested that women's support activities at that institution might provide a model of a general type:

> Basically, the model involves having women medical students organize and participate in three different organized groups: 1) a personal support and growth group; 2) a task-oriented group that works, in coordination with the administration of the medical school, toward identifying problem areas, developing constructive programs to rectify these problems, and programs that anticipate needs and serve a preventive rather than a curative function; and 3) a social-educational group.

At Irvine the task-oriented group is a:

> Committee on the Status on Women . . . which serves in an advisory capacity to the dean and concerns itself with a wide variety of tasks. These include recruiting women students and faculty; serving on the admissions committee; ensuring that there are women members of the faculty search committees, especially for such sensitive positions as the chairperson of the obstetrics and gynecology department; and arranging for women to be paired on clinical clerkships, since this opportunity, given the lack of female role models, helps overcome some of the difficulties of constantly being a minority.

The conferees agreed that women should create the means to communicate and take concerted action at the national level on matters important to them. Jacobs stressed the need for a data pool that could be consulted for information on women qualified for faculty and administrative posts when they become open. Driscoll, who is active in the Harvard Joint Committee, said that action in this area is in prospect. An agreement has been reached under which the publishers of *Who's Who in America* will collaborate with the Joint Committee in the preparation of a directory of women and minorities who are potential candidates for faculty and administrative positions in medicine and for appointment to advisory and policy-making bodies. Professional societies will be asked to communicate with their members, either by letter or by notice in their publications, requesting them to provide such information.

Action on a broad basis is also necessary to remedy the scarcity of women in leadership roles in medicine. Several conferees noted that the life goals of most women physicians do not include the occupation of leadership positions. Moreover, women in most cases lack the kind of experience that prepares men for top faculty and administrative posts.

Career Conflicts

A recurring theme throughout the conference was that the chief dilemma of women in medicine today is that they see themselves forced to choose between full commitment to a career and a satisfactory personal life; to choose, more specifically, between a career and having children.

One suggestion to help alleviate the problems of child care was embraced with considerable enthusiasm: Alice S. Cary of Doshiba Women's College in Kyoto, Japan, proposed that women physicians take the lead in developing training programs for domestic help that would include instruction in basic emergency medical and health care measures. The implication is that such programs would help make domestic employment more desirable by recognizing its importance.

For the foreseeable future, any woman physician who wishes to combine a career with marriage and motherhood will be well advised to find a spouse who is not only sympathetic to that aim, but willing to make the substantial supportive effort that is necessary. In the essential area of child care, the little research available seems to indicate that the mother with a "satisfactory" babysitter or housekeeper is, in most instances, one with a solid marriage and a satisfactory relationship with her children.

The pressures on women physicians through their period of professional development will presumably continue to be heavy, however medical education is organized. Roeske, reporting on research in which she has been engaged, said that the years of women physicians' training are marked by a series of "life conflicts." First there is the conflict of separation from the past and entry into the profession; then a feminine-masculine identity crisis arises when they seek to integrate a mixture of masculine and feminine role attributes as they assume the responsibilities of physicians; then the conflict of achieving full professional competence; and finally the conflict between a career and marriage and motherhood. Roeske said that a large majority of the women physicians studied said they could handle only one crisis at a time, with the result that most said they would defer childbearing until after residency training despite the risks this entails.

Special Capacity

One of the refrains of the discussion was that women have a special contribution to make to medicine because of a capacity for "nurturing," and because they are generally better than men in dealing with human relationships. Often, however, it seems that women in medical training are forced to choose between "compassion and competence." As Cary put it, women seem to have a special ear for relationships, but often "seem to be trained out of that ear." Thomas H. Meikle, Jr., of Cornell Medical College, and other conferees noted that the current image of the physician often results in unsatisfactory physician-patient relationships, particularly with women patients. Clinical education reinforces competition and aggression for women physicians and encourages an attitude inconsistent with their inherent compassion. Physicians need to learn to deal with patients as personal equals and the training of all physicians in more flexible attitudes should be a substantial issue in medical education.

Prospects for Change

While they cited a number of causes for concern, the conferees seemed, on balance, to be at least mildly optimistic about prospects for changes benefiting women physicians and, indeed, medicine generally. Shifts in public attitudes, such as those in favor of equalitarian marriage and of enhancement of the quality of life, are improving the chances for reform. And trends in federal legislation are expected to create an atmosphere in which new patterns of training and practice can be developed.

The conference did not produce a manifesto. Its message, rather, was that the gains of the recent past make it necessary to reexamine priorities and to move forward with new initiatives. Marilyn Heins of Wayne State University School of Medicine expressed this perception in concluding her account of research in which she had been engaged:

> I have learned from this study that both men and women doctors work too hard, and do not seem to have enough time for personal growth or for their families. After deep reflection, despite the title of the Macy conference, I think the problem is not women in medicine but the role of the physician. The expectation that self, school, and society have of the young physician should be looked at and studied. Are there models of training and practice patterns that achieve excellence of patient care without leading to the stresses of overwork that affect physicians—lack of time for self and family, alcoholism, drug abuse, suicide? Our profession should study itself carefully. . . . Mankind—humankind if you will—can choose. Scientific and objective self-study is the start of the process that leads to rational choice.

Background

Career Patterns

To give substance to a status report on women in medicine, several conference participants prepared papers that essentially documented the patterns of the careers of women physicians. At a time when changes in medicine are obviously occurring very rapidly it is risky to speak about career patterns as if they were immutable, but the data provided in these papers and in the McAnarney report provided a factual anchor for the discussion.

Just as women are underrepresented in leadership positions in American medical schools — there are no women deans; women assistant and associate deans tend to be limited to jobs dealing with students; and there are few women department chairmen — so have they also lagged in gaining other forms of peer recognition. Marion Kilson of the Radcliffe Institute noted that few women serve in top offices in national medical organizations, specialty societies, or major state or federal policy-making bodies.

Productivity

A sharply focused comparison of productivity was reported by Heins from a soon-to-be published study of men and women physicians in the Detroit area. Information on the equivalent of full-time work done since graduation from medical school indicated that all of the men and 17 percent of the women had worked more than 75 percent of the potential time they could have worked since graduation; only 9 percent of the women had worked less than half the potential time. Heins maintained the study showed that:

> The difference that does exist between men and women is the result of the time off from medical work that women take for childbearing and childrearing.

She also suggested that because women physicians are heavily represented in the primary care specialties, their productivity may be regarded as higher in that type of medical work, which is now in demand.

Results of productivity studies done in Britain and reported by Una Maclean of the University of Edinburgh paralleled these findings: the British research indicated that in terms of productivity unmarried women physicians pursue the same careers as men.

Maclean, incidentally, quoted research results that cast some doubt on the fairly widely held assumption that women whose mothers worked are more confident and better prepared to combine a medical career with motherhood. She cited a study of Glasgow women that

> . . . showed that as many as half had serious doubts about their being able to pursue a full-time medical career. The women most doubtful about being able to work later were, somewhat surprisingly, those who had a mother who worked.

Other Women in Health Care

While most of the discussion was pitched to a comparison between women physicians and their male peers there were references to the relationship of women doctors to other women in the health care field. At the conference, allusions to the "Navarro pyramid" became the shorthand reference to studies on the occupational and sex structure of the health labor force by Vincente Navarro and his colleagues at the Johns Hopkins University.[2]

According to the Navarro analysis, the health care industry is dominated by professionals belonging to the upper middle class. These are predominantly male physicians, but women physicians are included. The next tier is made up of nurses, therapists, and social workers, most of whom are lower-middle-class women. The base of the pyramid is composed largely of service workers, predominantly female, who are underpaid and poorly organized and unionized. Because most women physicians have been preoccupied with their difficulties in establishing conditions of equality with their male colleagues, they have not been fully aware of problems in their relationships with other women in the health care field.

The issue, as now foreseen, is that in pursuing their own career aims women physicians will find themselves increasingly at cross purposes with other women health workers. Women doctors may find that pursuit of some general goals — such as reducing hospital costs, which implies controlling employment — may clash with the interests of other women workers. Navarro's class analysis of the health care industry suggests that, in a showdown, professional ties will prove more important to women physicians than solidarity with other women, that class loyalties are stronger than sex loyalties. The testing of this hypothesis may well prove to be the next major challenge in store for women in medicine.

Notes

1. John S. Millis, *A Rational Public Policy for Medical Education and Its Financing.*
2. Vincente Navarro, "Women in Health Care," 398–402.

Career Patterns of
Women in Medicine
❧

Marjorie P. Wilson and Amber B. Jones*

The tasks of social change are tasks for the tough-minded and competent. Those who come to the task with the currently fashionable mixture of passion and incompetence only add to the confusion.

John Gardner[1]

Physicians often assume each of several socially valued roles: healer, counselor, teacher, and informed decision maker. Women who choose medicine as a career have selected a profession that allows them to affect significantly the quality of life around them.

In addition to meeting the demands of a multivariate professional role, a woman physician expects to assume the more traditional and equally demanding responsibilities of wife and mother. This combination of personal and professional obligations constitutes an awesome set of expectations. A framework in which to orchestrate these interdependent functions is a critical factor in the degree to which women physicians can achieve their fullest potential. We believe this framework must incorporate at least three key variables: 1) a clear vision of personal and professional life goals; 2) a broad knowledge and understanding of the forces, demands, and conditions imposed by the relevant social environment; and 3) access to substantive and political information of significance in the accomplishment of the multiple tasks.

After summarizing some of the retrospective data about

---

* Amber B. Jones, M.Ed., assistant director, Management Programs, Department of Institutional Development, Association of American Medical Colleges, did not attend the conference.

career patterns of women in medicine,[2] we will pose four key questions.

1. In 1974 women comprised 39.4 percent of the total labor force in the United States; 46.4 percent of all women of working age were employed (Table 1).

2. In the medical and health services industry, which employs over 4.2 million workers, the number of women increased from 65 to 75 percent in the twenty years from 1950 to 1970.

3. Among the 3.1 million persons in selected health occupations in 1970, the proportion of women ranged from 3.4 percent (dentists) to 97.9 percent (dental assistants) (Figure 1).

4. Thirty-five percent of women physicians and 57 percent

Table 1. Women in the Civilian Labor Force
in the United States: 1900–74

Year	Women in Labor Force (1,000s)	Women in Labor Force as Percent of	
		Total Labor Force	All Women of Working Age
1900	5,114	18.1	20.4
1910	7,889	20.9	25.2
1920	8,430	20.4	23.3
1930	10,679	22.0	24.3
1940	12,845	24.3	25.4
1945	19,270	29.6	35.7
1950	18,412	28.8	33.9
1955	20,584	30.2	35.7
1960	23,272	32.3	37.8
1965	26,232	34.0	39.3
1970	31,560	36.7	43.4
1972	33,320	37.4	43.8
1973	34,510	38.9	44.7
1974	35,825	39.4	46.4

SOURCE: For 1900–72, Women's Bureau, "The Economic Role of Women," reprinted from *Economic Report of the President, 1973* (Washington: U.S. Department of Labor, 1973): 9; for 1973 and 1974, Bureau of Labor Statistics, *Employment and Earnings* 21, no. 9 (Washington: U.S. Department of Labor, n.d.): 91.

NOTE: Reprinted with permission from *Women in Health Careers — Chart Book for the International Conference on Women in Health* (Washington: American Public Health Association, June 1975).

of men were in office-based practice; and 35 percent of women and 25 percent of men were in hospital-based practice.

5. In 1973 the northeast region of the United States had a significantly larger proportion of women physicians (Figure 2).

6. In 1973 the specialties of pediatrics (21.9 percent), anesthesiology (14.4 percent), pathology (14.0 percent), and psychiatry (13.7 percent) had the highest proportions of women (Table 2).

7. The largest numbers of women entered pediatrics (4,572), psychiatry (3,436), internal medicine (3,234), and general (family) practice (2,561) (Table 2).

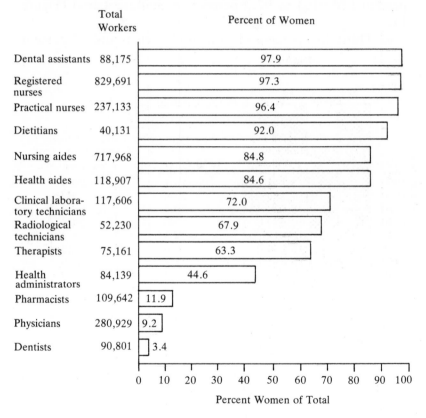

Figure 1. Women Workers in Selected Health Occupations: 1970.

NOTE: Reprinted with permission from *Women in Health Careers — Chart Book for the International Conference on Women in Health* (Washington: American Public Health Association, June 1975).

8. Data indicate that the more popular specialties for women physicians have the lowest net income for physicians of both sexes. The conclusion, based on a study of some fourteen hundred women and seven thousand men physicians, was that the average net income from medical practice in 1972 was $47,945 for men and $27,558 for women physicians, related in part to hours worked.

9. Women represented just under 15 percent of the total full-time faculty of American medical schools in 1971–72 and again in 1973–74; only a small percentage of women are at the

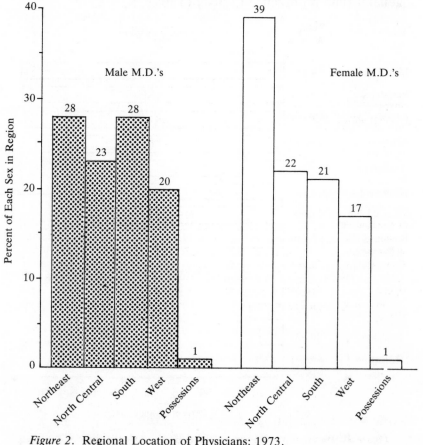

Figure 2. Regional Location of Physicians: 1973.

NOTE: Reprinted with permission from *Women in Health Careers — Chart Book for the International Conference on Women in Health* (Washington: American Public Health Association, June 1975).

Table 2. Primary Specialty of Active Physicians
in the United States, by Sex: 1973 and 1963

Specialty	Total	Male	Female	Percent Female
	1973			
All specialties	324,367	300,013	24,354	7.5
Anesthesiology	12,196	10,445	1,751	14.4
General (family) practice	53,946	51,385	2,561	4.5
Internal medicine	49,899	46,665	3,234	6.5
Obstetrics and gynecology	20,494	18,954	1,540	7.5
Pathology[a]	11,498	9,893	1,605	14.0
Pediatrics[a]	20,849	16,277	4,572	21.9
Psychiatry[a]	25,063	21,627	3,436	13.7
Radiology[a]	15,345	14,468	877	5.7
All other	115,077	110,299	4,778	19.6
	1963			
All specialties	261,728	246,771	14,957	5.7
Anesthesiology	7,639	6,622	1,017	13.3
General (family) practice	73,489	70,386	3,103	4.2
Internal medicine	34,742	33,229	1,513	4.4
Obstetrics and gynecology	15,720	14,807	913	5.8
Pathology[a]	7,347	6,664	683	9.3
Pediatrics[a]	14,207	11,602	2,605	18.3
Psychiatry[a]	16,581	14,642	1,939	11.7
Radiology[a]	8,751	8,422	329	3.8
All other	83,252	80,397	2,855	3.4

SOURCE: G. A. Roback, *Distribution of Physicians in the U.S., 1973.
Regional, State, County and Metropolitan Areas* (Chicago: American Medical
Association, 1974): 39, 47; C. N. Theodore, J. N. Haug, and B. C. Martin,
*Special Statistical Series—Selected Characteristics of the Physician Population,
1963 and 1967* (Chicago: American Medical Association, 1968): 33–34; and
AMA Center for Health Services Research and Development, Special Tabu-
lations on Women Physicians, 1973, AMA Physician Master File. Unpub-
lished.

NOTE: Reprinted with permission from *Women in Health Careers—Chart
Book for the International Conference on Women in Health* (Washington:
American Public Health Association, June 1975).

[a] Includes subspecialties.

professor or associate professor level (Table 3).

10. Although it is usually assumed that many more women
faculty are employed on a part-time basis as compared to men,
the difference is perhaps not that striking (Table 4).

11. For every medical school class between 1940 and 1970,

Table 3. Employment Characteristics of Medical School Faculties in the United States, by Sex: 1971 and 1974

Characteristic	Total	Male	Female	Percent Female
	1973–74			
All faculty members	37,180[a]	31,623	5,438	14.6
Degree				
M.D.	24,342	21,952	2,325	9.5
Ph.D.	9,626	8,229	1,378	14.3
Other	3,212	1,442	1,735	54.6
Department				
Basic sciences or clinical specialties	35,431	30,500	4,816	15.3
Library	218	58	160	73.3
Allied health	658	286	370	56.4
Administration	500	460	39	7.8
All other	373	319	53	14.2
	1971–72			
All faculty members	34,658[b]	29,499	5,046	14.6
Degree				
M.D.	22,615	20,512	2,041	9.0
Non-M.D.'s	12,043	8,987	3,005	25.1
Department				
Basic sciences or clinical specialties	32,874	28,362	4,405	13.7
Library	230	66	164	71.3
Allied health	648	260	386	59.6
Administration	532	495	35	6.6
All other	374	316	56	15.0
	Percentage distribution 1970–71			
Faculty members reporting	28,452[c]	23,143	3,858	
Academic rank	100[d]	100	100	
Professor	23	96	4	
Associate professor	23	91	9	
Assistant professor	34	84	16	
Instructor	14	69	31	
Associate	3	68	32	
Assistant	[e]	61	39	
Lecturer	[e]	63	37	
No academic rank	1	88	12	

SOURCE: Association of American Medical Colleges, Division of Operation Studies, data on distribution of full-time and part-time salaried faculty in United States medical schools by sex and ethnic group, 1973–74 (unpublished); see also unpublished data for 1971–72; and National Institutes of Health, *Profiles of U.S. Medical Schools Faculty, 1971,* Resources of Biomedical Research Report No. 20 (Washington: U. S. Department of Health, Education, and Welfare, 1974).

Table 4. United States Medical School Faculty Holding the M.D., 1973–74

| | Nature of Employment (Percent) | |
	Male	Female
Strict full-time	64	61
Geographic full-time	21	19
Part-time	15	20
Total	100	100

SOURCE: Philip Anderson, *Descriptive Study of Salaried Medical School Faculty,* (Washington: Association of American Medical Colleges, December 1975): Table 31-C, 72.

except those of 1945 and 1946, a greater proportion of the women than of the men graduated were on medical school faculties[3] (Figure 3).

First-year enrollment of women medical students reached 23.8 percent in 1975–76.[4] In 1976, twenty-one medical schools had at least 30 percent of women in entering classes.

Other findings have been relatively consistent in a number of studies in the past decade.[5] Women physicians marry in the same proportion as women generally, but they marry later in life and tend to have fewer children. Over half are married to physicians.[6] About one-third of women physicians have fixed salary/fixed hour appointments, compared to 15 percent of men; 63 percent of women are not board certified compared to 49 percent of men.

The studies of the late 1960s showed that almost 91 percent of women physicians remained active on a full- or part-time basis. All studies showed that the number of hours per year

NOTE: Reprinted with permission from *Women in Health Careers — Chart Book for the International Conference on Women in Health* (Washington: American Public Health Association, June 1975).

[a] Male and females will not always add to total faculty, due to 119 faculty who did not indicate their sex in survey.

[b] Male and females will not always add to total faculty, due to 113 faculty who did not indicate their sex in survey.

[c] Excludes 1,451 faculty whose sex or major activity was not reported.

[d] Percentages may not add to 100 due to rounding.

[e] Less than 0.5 percent.

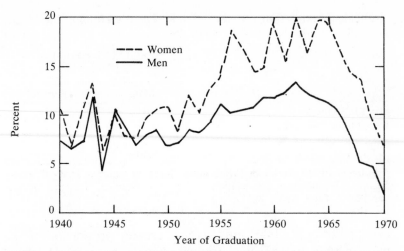

Figure 3. Proportions of Men and Women United States Medical Graduates (Classes of 1940–1970) on Medical School Faculties in 1975 (Full- and Part-Time, All Ranks).

SOURCE: H. Paul Jolly and Thomas A. Larson, "Datagram: Women Physicians on U.S. Medical School Faculties," *Journal of Medical Education* 50 (August 1975): 825.

worked by women is substantially less than men, but Lee Powers makes the point that this may be partially related to the nature of the positions they hold.[7] Phoebe A. Williams's study of Radcliffe women showed that two-thirds worked more than thirty-five hours a week and many worked more than sixty.[8] A 1975 study by Judith Jussim and Charlotte Muller calculated the average time spent in practice by women to be 32.6 years, and for men, 35.8.[9]

These statistics present no new or original data, but make the following points clear:

- Women predominate in the work force in the *health field*.
- They are generally paid less than men.
- They hold fewer top-level positions.
- The enrollment of women in medicine is now significantly greater than ever.
- A greater proportion of women medical graduates enter academic medicine than men graduates.
- Women do frequently combine a career and family life.

We will now focus on four issues, posed as questions, which we believe involve forces that will modulate the careers of women physicians in the future.

Question 1. Will the proportion of women physicians ever reach the proportion of women in the general population?

A Delphi survey[10] of the Council of Deans of United States medical schools, administered by the Association of American Medical Colleges, predicted that, by 1985, 30 percent of the physician population would be women.[11] We believe that proportion will be reached, but doubt that women will be represented in medicine to the same extent as they are in the general population. As long as the present economic structure exists, the male domination of the profession will be slow to change. The possibility of a national health insurance program would bring far more regulation to medicine, however, and it would probably be less attractive to those whom the dollar drives; the proportion of women in medicine may therefore increase further.

Question 2. Do women physicians want leadership roles? Can women doctors attain a fair share of managerial and executive positions in the future in proportion to their numbers in the work force?

To reflect for a moment on what leadership means, Douglas McGregor states that many characteristics alleged to be essential turn out not to differentiate the successful leader per se.[12] In fact some of these—integrity, ambition, judgment, for example—are to be found in any successful member of an organization.

The marks of success, as well as of leadership, for women physicians may simply be to maintain high standards of professional care; to practice with compassion; and to work in specialties of their choice. Can women physicians provide some of the answers to the type of criticism of the current approach to medical care that Ivan Illich's controversial book *Medical Nemesis* raises?[13] The disaffected public reflects some of the same dissatisfaction. Even though the number of women physicians in the total health services work force may always remain relatively small, they *can* have an enormous influence on the quality of life in the general population through their standards of practice and their approach to their work.

In studies of women Ph.D.'s there is evidence that challenges M.S. Horner's achievement motivation theories, based on the concepts that women fear and avoid success.[14] There is no denying the fact that senior administrative positions are rarely occupied by women. We do not believe, however, it is fear of success or of failure that has kept women from executive positions in medicine. One possible explanation is that the older generation of women physicians entered medicine with the principal career goal of setting up an independent practice. As a result their effort was focused on the care of individual patients rather than on lobbying for personal status in organizations. In the past two or three years a number of women have indicated an interest in managerial roles, and some have been thrust into positions of major administrative responsibility. The notion of aspiring to these roles has come to them relatively late in their careers; they should have been on a different career track long ago in order to be groomed for positions such as chairperson, dean, vice-president, hospital president, or trustee. Job changes have been made in the absence of any clearly articulated career goal. As a result there is generally no pattern of experience among women physicians linked to progressively responsible leadership posts. This uneven career development has provided a justification for denying women positions with real growth potential.

A recent American Public Health Association study of communication networks in the professional communities suggests that formal and informal channels of communication play a crucial role in the career development process.[15] Professional recognition is crucial to both vertical and horizontal mobility within a field. Women have had differential access to the colleague system, to the sponsor-protegé relationship, and, in the past, to committee memberships through appointment or election, particularly in professional associations.

In discussing leadership and the development of managerial

talent, McGregor makes the point that growth of the individual depends heavily on the environment in which that person works; he believes that the individual will grow into what she or he is capable of becoming, provided the proper conditions are created for that growth. McGregor describes a process of self-development leading to the realization of the individual's potentialities.[16] Perhaps another area in which we can work, therefore, is to help create the proper conditions for growth for women in the professional environment and to provide assistance in the process of self-development. We have no doubt, for example, that physicians in administrative positions need to acquire knowledge of and facility in using managerial tools. This is one area in which we can speak from experience, because over the past five years the American Association of Medical Colleges has sponsored an executive development program for senior medical school administrators. They learn how to run effective meetings; to work with small and large groups of people; to manage conflict; and to set goals, objectives, priorities, and criteria for success. They learn quite a lot about fiscal management, and are given advice about how to manage their time and about the use and misuse of management information systems, computers, forecasting, and modeling. Few women physicians have had an opportunity to participate in such training sessions, however, as not many occupy senior decision-making positions.

Question 3. How can women physicians cope with the superwoman roles of combining a career and family?

Professional careers are not a substitute or a partial tradeoff, but an addition to the role of the mother-wife-homemaker. It *is* surprising to find that "superwoman" does not lament her lot in life, per se. The question is: Does it present a hazard for the profession and for the family? How can we help competent and dedicated women to fulfill effectively the multiple roles they assume? If women expect special consideration in terms of working hours and/or conditions, can they expect to be appointed to demanding leadership positions? While it is true that the overworked male physician is a subject for careful study and serious concern, it is also true that those men who have succeeded in executive positions have devoted an inordinate amount of time and energy to their work.

Perhaps the most effective way to deal with the superwoman phenomenon is to devise ways to ease those burdens the woman professional need *not* bear, so that she can concentrate her energy on the aspects of her work and family life that only she can do. The conflicts that arise are often representative of role overload and time bonds rather than an indication of any intrinsic functional incompatibility. More equitable salaries, more favorable tax laws, and models of sharing personal resources among women with like concerns can, for example, stretch the ability to purchase needed services and time-saving procedures and devices. A mutually supportive network of women in academic medicine has been suggested as a means to facilitate access to necessary professional information; a more personal support network might be equally important: access to the body of knowledge about setting personal life goals; time management; and other coping strategies could be enormously helpful.

We are all aware that a critical issue for the professional woman is the potential influence of her behavior on her family, particularly her children. In preparing this paper we thought at length about the responsibilities of a good parent. Our conclusion is that the quality of life issues within the family are not exclusively female or motherhood responsibilities, although women professionals may tend to regard them as if they *were* exclusively theirs, and not necessarily shared responsibilities, and so they may feel guilty accordingly.

Question 4. Do women physicians understand and can they deal with the hostility among large numbers of women health workers toward male physicians and administrators who dominate the health services industry?

This is perhaps the most critical question of all. A year ago the International Conference on Women in Health reflected in no uncertain terms the growing assertiveness among women health workers of all types. It is not all sweetness and light; our call for quality performance among women physicians is not that we go forth simply as a gaggle of do-gooders. (We refer you to the quotation from John Gardner at the beginning of this paper.) The international conference reflected a growing realization among women health care providers that not only must there be changes in the distribution of women within the medical industry hierarchy, but the hierarchy itself must be reconstructed. The conference atmosphere was highly charged, and the hostility directed toward physicians, particularly, was arresting. Women health professionals do not want merely to take men's places, to act as men do, and to become the dominant rather than the dominated. As women, they are concerned not only with improving the status and representation of women as providers of health care, but with broader goals. In spite of the underlying resentment of physicians, however, recommendations were made at the conference for ways to increase the number of women physicians.

We believe women physicians can make a tremendous contribution toward improving professional and working relationships between physicians and nurses and among other health professionals. As pointed out earlier, 75 percent of the total health services work force is female.

We shall paraphrase a few thoughts from the international conference to indicate the flavor of the meeting:

1. Participants acknowledged that the greatest proportion of health care is provided within families — by mothers and daughters; it was recommended that skills be taught in a manner that would decrease dependency on impersonal professional services and increase the competence of female family members to provide first-line care in the home.

2. Participants discussed what it was like to receive health care services from "alien and alienating providers." It was recommended that citizen groups be given a determining voice in the selection of health care trainees, including physicians, in order to influence the attitudes of future health professionals.

3. Participants wanted to redirect training programs, as well as the manner in which health care services are provided for

mothers and their children. The view was expressed that push-ing highly credentialed women into showcase jobs sometimes coopted these women. It was therefore recommended that the cause of the conferees be represented in policy-determining positions by women "from their ranks, empowered by their constituency."

Vincente Navarro believes that the appointment of women to positions of power in institutions will be a necessary but not sufficient condition to improve the situation of the majority of women in the health sector; he summarizes by saying that the betterment of a few does not imply, nor does it necessarily result in, the betterment of the many.[17] If women physicians are to be instruments of change in the health care field they must understand the social, political, and economic forces involved.

Another group of women working to improve the status and responsibilities of women as providers of health care have formalized a series of objectives for accomplishing their goals. Three are of particular relevance:

1. Increase the percentage of women physicians in the United States to a minimum of 25 percent of all physicians by 1986.

2. Increase the number of entering female students to at least 45 percent by 1986.

3. Increase the number of women in decision-making posi-tions in the health care delivery system, in academic institu-tions, and within federal, state, and local agencies by expand-ing the number of women in management positions in the health field (government and private) by at least 20 percent in 1986.[18]

There are clearly some contradictions and conflicts around the possible answers to the four questions we have posed. Whatever directions women physicians seek in their careers in the future, a great deal of help can be provided to assure their success and relieve their stress. Access to needed information can be given through networks of women physicians and other professionals. The dissemination of appropriate literature and the convening of workshops and seminars can enhance the quality of their contributions in all aspects of their professional and family lives.

We would suggest that we are moving into a fourth era that can be added to what Marion Kilson of the Radcliffe Institute calls the three phases of formation, consolidation, and reintegration. There is no precise descriptor for this next phase of development, but it will be characterized by far greater attention to the human values of our culture. Will women physicians display greater humanity in the care of their patients, in their treatment of each other, and in their behavior within organizations and in the community?

If they are to have a determining influence, there must be more dialogue among thoughtful and mature women about the future role of women physicians during this era of change. We must be clear about our values and what we stand for, and we must have a set of goals and some pragmatic achievable objectives for the coming years. There can and should be an organized effort to develop the leadership talent among women physicians, which the medical profession and our country need.

Notes

1. John Gardner has served as secretary of the U.S. Department of Health, Education, and Welfare and until recently chaired the citizens' lobby, Common Cause.
2. Maryland Pennell and Shirlene Showell, *Women in Health Careers*.
3. H. Paul Jolly and Thomas Larson, "Women Physicians on U.S. Medical School Faculties," 825–27.
4. W. F. Dubé, "Women Enrollment and Its Minority Component in U.S. Medical School Faculties," 691–93.
5. See for example: Roscoe A. Dykman and John M. Stalmaker, "Survey of Women Physicians Graduating from Medical School, 1925–40," 3–38; John Z. Bowers, "Women in Medicine," 362–65; Mary Loretta Rosenlund and Frank A. Oski, "Women in Medicine," 1008–12; Carol Lopate, *Women in Medicine*, 10–93; Margie R. Matthews, *Women Physicians in Training and Practice*; Charles E. Phelps, "Women in American Medicine,"

916–24; Carol S. Shapiro, Barbara-Jean Stibler, Audrey A. Zelkovic, and Judith Mausner, "Careers of Women Physicians," 1033–40; Phoebe A. Williams, "Women in Medicine," 584–91.

6. Dykman and Stalmaker, "Survey of Women Physicians" (see note 5).
7. Lee Powers, Rexford C. Parmelle, and Harry Wisenfelder, "Preliminary Report: Practice Patterns of Women and Men Physicians."
8. Williams, "Women in Medicine" (see note 5).
9. Judith Jussim and Charlotte Muller, "Medical Education for Women," 572–79.
10. T. J. Gordon and O. Helmer, *Report on a Long-Range Forecasting Study.*
11. Joseph A. Keyes, Marjorie P. Wilson, and Jane Becker, "The Future of Medical Education," 319–27.
12. Douglas McGregor, *The Human Side of Enterprise.*
13. Ivan Illich, *Medical Nemesis.*
14. M. S. Horner, "Feminity and Successful Achievement."
15. Patricia A. Yokopenic, Linda Brookover Bourque, and Donna Brogan, in *Social Problems,* 493–509.
16. McGregor, *Human Side* (see note 12).
17. Vincente Navarro, "Women in Health Care," 398–402.
18. Women's Action Alliance, "Report to the Task Force in Health and Physical Safety."

Bibliography

"A Married Doctress." *Philadelphia Medical Times* 1 (1871): 187.

Alsop, Gulielma Fell. *History of the Woman's Medical College, Philadelphia, Pennsylvania, 1850–1950.* Philadelphia: J. B. Lippincott Co., 1950.

Altman, Lawrence K. "Malpractice Crisis Overshadows Agenda as A.M.A. Session Opens." *New York Times* (15 June 1975): 44.

Anderson, Philip. *Descriptive Study of Salaried Medical School Faculty.* Washington: Association of American Medical Colleges, 1975.

American Medical Association Center for Health Services Research and Development. Special Tabulations on Women Physicians, 1973, AMA Physician Master File. Unpublished. Chicago: American Medical Association, 1973.

Association News. "Council on Community Health Seeks Facts on Women Dropouts." *Canadian Medical Association Journal* 114 (7 February 1976).

Association of American Medical Colleges, Division of Operational Studies. Data on distribution of full-time and part-time salaried faculty in U.S. medical schools by sex and ethnic group, 1973–74. Unpublished. See also unpublished data for 1971–72.

―――. *Participation of Women and Minorities on U.S. Medical School Faculties.* Washington: Association of American Medical Colleges, 1976.

Austin, Margaret. "History of Women in Medicine: A Symposium; Early Period." *Bulletin of the Medical Library Association* 44 (January 1956): 12–15.

Baker, R. *The First Woman Doctor—The Story of Elizabeth Blackwell, M.D.* New York: Julian Messner, Inc., 1944.

Bardwick, Judith M. "Psychological Conflict and the Reproductive System." In *Feminine Personality and Conflict,* edited by J. M. Bardwick; E. Douvan; M. S. Horner; and D. Gutman. Belmont, California: Brooks/Cole, 1970.

Baum, Allyn Z. "Is Medical Training Wasted on Women?" *Medical Economics* 46 (December 1969): 100–07.

Bayer, A. E., and Astin, H. S. "Sex Differentials in the Academic Reward System." *Science* 188 (1975): 796.

Blake, John B. "Women and Medicine in Ante-Bellum America."

Bulletin of the History of Medicine 39, no. 2. (March–April 1965): 99–123.

Blitz, Rudolph C. "Women in the Professions, 1870–1970." *Monthly Labor Review* 97 (May 1974): 34–39.

Bowers, John Z. "Women in Medicine." *New England Journal of Medicine* 275 (18 August 1966): 362–65.

Braunwald, Eugene. "Future Shock in Academic Medicine." *New England Journal of Medicine* 286 (11 May 1972): 1031–35.

Buck, C.; Scoffield, M.; and Warwick, O. H. "A Survey of Women Graduates from a Canadian Medical School." *Canadian Medical Association Journal* 94 (2 April 1966).

Campbell, Margaret A. *Why Would a Girl Go into Medicine?* Old Westbury, New York: Feminist Press, 1973.

Cartwright, L. K. "The Personality and Family Background of a Sample of Women Medical Students at the University of California." *Journal of the American Medical Women's Association* 27 (1962): 260–66.

Chadwick, James R. *The Study and Practice of Medicine by Women.* New York: A. S. Barnes & Co., 1879.

Cohen, Eva D., and Korper, Samuel P. "Women in Medicine: A Survey of Professional Activities, Career Interruptions, and Conflict Resolutions. Trends in Career Patterns." *Connecticut Medicine* 40 (1976): 195–200.

"Discrimination Widespread: Being Female Still a Handicap to M.D.'s." *American Medical News* (17 November 1975): 1.

Drouilhet, Elizabeth. "The Fifty Years of Vassar I Have Seen." *Spring At Vassar* (June 1976).

Dubé, W. F. "Women Enrollment and its Minority Component in U.S. Medical Schools." *Journal of Medical Education* 51 (August 1976): 691–93.

Dubé, W. F., and Johnson, Davis G. "Datagram: Study of U.S. Medical School Applicants, 1973–74." *Journal of Medical Education* 50 (November 1975): 1015–32.

Dykman, Roscoe A., and Stalmaker, John M. "Survey of Women Physicians Graduating from Medical School 1925–1940." *Journal of Medical Education* 32, pt. 2 (March 1957): 3–38.

"Economic Role of Women." Reprinted from *Economic Report of the President.* Washington: U.S. Department of Labor, 1973.

Epstein, Cynthia Fuchs. *Woman's Place: Options and Limits in Professional Careers.* Berkeley: University of California Press, 1970.

Exploratory Study of Women in the Health Professions Schools. Vols.

I–X. Mimeographed. Washington: United States Department of Health, Education, and Welfare, September 1976. Volume X is an extensive annotated bibliography.

Ferrell, Tom, and Johnston, Donald. "Medicare Fraud." *New York Times,* (1 August 1976): E7.

Friedman, Richard C.; Kornfeld, Donald S.; and Bigger, Thomas J. "Psychological Problems Associated with Sleep Deprivation in Interns." *Journal of Medical Education* 48 (May 1973): 436–41.

Friedson, Eliot. *Profession of Medicine.* New York: Dodd, Mead & Co., 1970.

Fruen, Mary A.: Robhan, Arthur I.; and Steiner, Jan W. "Comparison of Characteristics of Male and Female Medical School Applicants." *Journal of Medical Education* 49 (February 1974): 137–45.

"Gallup Survey" (on doctors' competency). *New York Times* (15 June 1975): 44.

"Gallup Survey" (on medicine as professional choice). *New York Times* (2 December 1973): 50.

The Gallup Opinion Index, Report No. 128. *Women in America.* Princeton: American Institute of Public Opinion, March 1976.

Garfinkle, Stuart H. "Occupations of Women and Black Workers, 1962–74." *Monthly Labor Review* 98 (November 1975): 25–35.

Geertsma, Robert H., and Grinols, Donald R. "Specialty Choice in Medicine." *Journal of Medical Education* 47 (July 1972): 509–17.

Ginzberg, Eli. *Life Styles of Educated Women.* New York: Columbia University Press, 1966.

Goldstein, Marion Zucker. "Preventive Mental Health Efforts for Women Medical Students." *Journal of Medical Education* 50 (March 1975): 289–91.

Gordon, T. J., and Helmer, O. *Report on a Long-Range Forecasting Study.* Report No. P. 2982. Santa Monica, California: Rand Corporation, 1964.

Graham, Patricia Albjerg. "Women in Academic Life." In *Women and Success: The Anatomy of Achievement,* edited by Ruth B. Kundsin. New York: William Morrow & Co., 1974: 238–47.

————. "So Much To Do: Guides for Historical Research on Women in Higher Education." *Teachers College Record* 76 (February 1975): 421–29.

Gray, Robert M.; Newman, W. R. Elton; and Reinhardt, Adina M. "The Effect of Medical Specialization on Physicians' Attitudes." *Journal of Health and Human Behavior* 7, no. 2 (Summer 1966): 128–32.

Gross, Wendy, and Cronitz, Elaine. "A Comparison of Medical

Students' Attitudes towards Women and Women Medical Students." *Journal of Medical Education* 50 (April 1975): 392–94.

Hacker, C. *The Indomitable Lady Doctors.* N.p.: Irwin and Co., 1974.

Hall, Oswald. "The Stages of a Medical Career." *American Journal of Sociology* 53 (March 1948): 327–36.

Hall, P. Q.; Malcolm, S. M.; and Posner, S. E. "Conference on Minority Women Scientists." *Science* 191 (1976): 457.

Haller, John S., Jr. "Neurasthenia." *New York State Journal of Medicine* (1971): 473–81.

Hanaford, Phebe A. *Daughters of America; or Women of the Century.* Augusta, Maine: True & Co., 1883.

Harvard University Joint Committee on the Status of Women at Harvard Medical School, Harvard School of Dental Medicine, and Harvard School of Public Health. "Annual Report of the Joint Committee on the Status of Women, 1973–74." Mimeographed. Boston: Harvard Medical School, Harvard School of Dental Medicine, Harvard School of Public Health, September 1974.

———. "Annual Report of the Joint Committee on the Status of Women, 1974–75." Mimeographed. Boston: Harvard Medical School, Harvard School of Dental Medicine, Harvard School of Public Health, September 1975.

———. "Obstacles to Equal Education at Harvard Resulting from Sex Discrimination. A Report of the Task Force." Mimeographed. Boston: Harvard Medical School, Harvard School of Dental Medicine, Harvard School of Public Health, July 1974.

———. "Report of the Student Task Force (HMS) of the Joint Committee." Mimeographed. Boston: Harvard Medical School, Harvard School of Dental Medicine, Harvard School of Public Health, September 1975.

———. "Institutions Offering Reduced-Schedule Training, Revised Listing." Mimeographed. Boston: Harvard Medical School, Harvard School of Dental Medicine, Harvard School of Public Health, April 1976.

Harris, Louis and Associates. *1972 Virginia Slims American Women's Opinion Poll.* New York: Philip Morris, 1972.

Hart, E. W., and Diridoni, P. W. "Status of Staff Women and Minorities at the University of California at San Francisco." (San Francisco: University of California, 1975).

Heins, Marilyn; Smock, Sue; Jacobs, Jennifer; and Stein, Margaret. "Productivity of Women Physicians." *Journal of the American Medical Association* 236, no. 17 (25 October 1976): 1961–64.

Helsop, Barbara F.; Molloy, Robyn J.; Waal-Manning, Hendrika J., et al. "Women in Medicine in New Zealand." *New Zealand Medical Journal* 77 (1973): 219–29.

Hilberman, Elaine; Konanc, Judy; Perez-Reyes, Marcia, et al. "Support Groups for Women in Medical School: A First-Year Program." *Journal of Medical Education* 50 (September 1975): 867–75.

Holton, Susan Chapin. "The Woman Physician: A Study of Role Conflict." *Journal of the American Medical Women's Association* 24 (1969): 638–45.

Horner, M. S. "Femininity and Successful Achievement: A Basic Inconsistency." In *Feminine Personality and Conflict,* edited by Judith M. Bardwick, E. Douvan, M. S. Horner, and D. Gutman. Belmont, California: Brooks/Cole, 1970.

Howell, Mary C. "What Medical Schools Teach about Women." *New England Journal of Medicine* 291 (8 August 1974): 304–07.

———. "Can We Be Feminist Physicians? Mirages, Dilemmas and Traps." Paper delivered at University of California, Irvine, Conference on Women in Medicine, 14 February 1976.

Howell, Mary C., and Hiatt, D. "Do Women Student Health Services Discriminate Against Women: A Survey of Services in the U.S. Medical Schools." *Journal of the American College Health Association* 23 (1975): 867.

Hurd-Mead, Kate Campbell. *Medical Women of America: A Short History of the Pioneer Medical Women of America and a Few of Their Colleagues in England.* New York: Froben Press, 1933.

Hutchins, E. "Minorities, Manpower and Medicine." Technical Report No. S 633. Evanston, Illinois: Association of American Medical Colleges, 1966.

Jacobi, Mary Putnam. "Women in Medicine." In *Woman's Work in America,* edited by Annie Nathan Meyer. New York: Henry Holt Co., 1891: 139–205.

Johnson, Davis, G. "The Medical Student, 1975." In *Recent Trends in Medical Education,* edited by Elizabeth F. Purcell. New York: Josiah Macy, Jr. Foundation, 1976: 37–53.

Johnson, Davis G., and Hutchins, Edwin B. "Doctor or Dropout: A Study of Medical Student Attrition." *Journal of Medical Education* 41 (December 1966): 1107–40.

Jolly, H. Paul, and Larson, Thomas A. "Datagram: Women Physicians on U.S. Medical Faculties." *Journal of Medical Education* 50 (August 1975): 825–27.

———. *Participation of Women and Minorities on U.S. Medical*

School Faculties. Washington: Association of American Medical Colleges, 1976.

Jussim, Judith, and Muller, Charlotte. "Medical Education for Women: How Good an Investment?" *Journal of Medical Education* 50 (June 1975): 572–79.

Kaiser, Barbara L., and Kaiser, Irvin H. "The Challenge of the Women's Movement to American Gynecology." *American Journal of Obstetrics and Gynecology* 120, no. 5 (1 November 1974): 652–65.

Kaplan, Harold. "Part-Time Residency Training; An Approach to the Graduate Training of Some Women Physicians." *Journal of the American Medical Women's Association* 27 (1972): 648–50.

Keyes, Joseph A.; Wilson, Marjorie P.; and Becker, Jane. "The Future of Medical Education: Forecast of the Council of Deans." *Journal of Medical Education* 50 (April 1975): 319–27.

Kobrin, Frances E. "The American Midwife Controversy: A Crisis of Professionalization." *Bulletin of the History of Medicine* 40, no. 4 (July–August 1966): 350–65.

Korcok, M., and Geekie, D. A. "Report Issued by Requirements Subcommittee of National Committee on Physician Manpower." *Canadian Medical Association Journal* 115 (7 August 1976).

Kosa, John. "Women and Medicine in a Changing World." In *The Professional Woman,* edited by Athena Theodore. Cambridge, Massachusetts: Schenkman, 1971: 709–19.

Lake, Karen. "Personality Inventories: A Study of Medical Students." Unpublished data. N.p., August 1976.

Lamarche, G., and Deschenes, S. M. "Medical School Enrollment." *Association of Canadian Medical Colleges* ix, no. 1 (January–February 1976).

Lieberman, Jethro; Mims, Bob; and Wollman, Bill. "The Troubled Professions." *Business Week* (16 August 1976): 126–38.

Lopate, Carol. *Women in Medicine.* Baltimore: Published for the Josiah Macy, Jr. Foundation by Johns Hopkins Press, 1968.

Lorber, Judith. "Women and Medical Sociology: Invisible Professionals and Ubiquitous Patients." In *Another Voice,* edited by Marcia Millman and Rosabeth Moss Kanter. Garden City, New York: Anchor Books, 1975: 75–105.

Lovejoy, Esther Pohl. *Women Doctors of the World.* New York: Macmillan Co., 1957.

Lowther, Florence de L., and Downes, Helen R. "Women in Medicine." *Journal of the American Medical Association* 129, no. 7 (13 October 1945): 512–14.

Macdonald, E. M., and Webb, E. M. "A Survey of Women Physicians in Canada, 1883-1964." *Canadian Medical Association Journal* 94 (4 June 1966).

Maclean, Una. *Social and Community Medicine for Students*. N.p.: Heinemann, 1971.

Mandelbaun, D. R. "Toward an Understanding of the Career Persistence of Women Physicians." *Journal of the American Medical Women's Association* 31 (1976): 314-24.

Matlin, Margaret W. "Sex Ratios in Authorship and Acknowledgments for Medical Journal Articles." *Journal of the American Medical Women's Association* 29 (1974): 173-74.

Matthews, Margie R. *Women Physicians in Training and Practice*. Durham: Duke University Medical Center, 1968.

———. "The Training and Practice of Women Physicians." *Journal of Medical Education* 45 (December 1970): 173-74.

McGrath, E. "Women from Two Medical Schools: Differences in Backgrounds, Attitudes and Personalities." Submitted to *Journal of Medical Education*, July 1976.

McGrath, E., and Zinnet, C. N. "Female and Male Medical Students: Differences in Specialty Choice: Specialty Beliefs and Personality Characteristics. In preparation, 1976.

McGregor, Douglas. *The Human Side of Enterprise*. New York: McGraw Hill Book Co., 1960.

McGrew, Elizabeth A. History of Women in Medicine; A Symposium: The Present: *Bulletin of the Medical Library Association* 44 (January 1956): 23-24.

Mead, Kate Campbell. "Women Have Arrived." *Medical Economics* 13 (January 1936): 23-26.

Means, James Howard. "Homo Medicus Americanus." *Daedalus* 92 (Fall 1963): 701-23.

"Medical Education in the United States 1968-1969." *Journal of the American Medical Association 69th Annual Report* 210, no. 8 (24 November 1969): 1456-1579.

"Medical Education in the United States 1970-1971." *Journal of the American Medical Association 71st Annual Report* 218, no. 8 (22 November 1971): 1200-85.

"Medical Education in the United States 1974-1975." *Journal of the American Medical Association 75th Annual Report* 234, no. 13 (29 December 1975): 1325-99.

"Medical Education in the United States 1975-1976." *Journal of the American Medical Association 76th Annual Report* 236, no. 26 (27 December 1976): 2949-3040.

Medical School Admission Requirements 1977–78. Washington: Association of American Medical Colleges, 1976.

Miller, Deborah W. "Where There Is a Will There Is a Way." *Harvard Medical Alumni Bulletin* 50 (September–October 1975): 19.

Millis, John S. *A Rational Public Policy for Medical Education and Its Financing.* New York: National Fund for Medical Education, 1971.

Morgan, Beverly C. "Admission of Women into Medical Schools in the United States." *Woman Physician* 26 (1971): 305–09.

Morrow, Laura E. "Statistics on Women in Medicine and Addendum to Publicity and Public Relations. 1972 Annual Report." *Journal of the American Medical Women's Association* 28 (1973): 600–02.

Mount, J. H., and Fish, David G. "Canadian Medical Student Interest in General Practice and the Specialties." *Canadian Medical Association Journal* 94 (2 April 1966).

Mumford, Emily. *Interns: From Students to Physicians.* Cambridge: Harvard University Press, 1970.

Nadelson, Carol, and Notman, Malkah. "The Woman Physician." *Journal of Medical Education* 47 (March 1972): 176–83.

———. "Medicine: A Career Conflict for Women." *American Journal of Psychiatry* 130 (1973): 1123–27.

———. "Success or Failure: Women as Medical School Applicants." *Journal of the American Medical Women's Association* 29 (1974): 167–72.

National Institutes of Health, *Profiles of U.S. Medical Schools Faculty, 1971,* Resources of Biomedical Research Report No. 20 (Washington: U.S. Department of Health, Education, and Welfare, 1974).

Navarro, Vincente. "Women in Health Care." *New England Journal of Medicine* 292 (20 February 1975) 398–402.

Nelson-Jones, Richard, and Fish, David G. "Women Students in Canadian Medical Schools." *British Journal of Medical Education* 4 (1970): 97–108.

Nemir, Rosa Lee. "AMWA—Six Decades of Progress (in the Service of Women in Medicine)." *Journal of the American Medical Women's Association* 29 (1974): 486–91.

Oakley, Ann. "The Family, Marriage and Its Relationship to Illness." In *An Introduction to Medical Sociology,* edited by David Tuckett. London: Tavistock, 1976.

Ortiz, Flora Ida. "Women and Medicine: The Process of Professional

Incorporation." *Journal of the American Medical Women's Association* 30 (1975): 18-30.

Parrish, John B. "Women in Professional Training." *Monthly Labor Review* 97 (May 1974): 42-43.

Pennell, Maryland Y., and Renshaw, Josephine E. "Distribution of Women Physicians." *Journal of the American Medical Women's Association* 27 (1972): 197-203.

Pennell, Maryland, and Showell, Shirlene. *Women in Health Careers — Chart Book for the International Conference on Women in Health.* Washington: American Public Health Association, June 1975.

Phelps, Charles E. "Women in American Medicine." *Journal of Medical Education* 43 (August 1968): 916-24.

Pierrel, Rosemary. "Medical Career Interests Among College Women." *Journal of the American Medical Women's Association* 19 (1964): 135-38.

Powers, Lee; Parmelle, Rexford C.; and Wisenfelder, Harry. "Preliminary Report: Practice Patterns of Women and Men Physicians." Mimeographed. Josiah Macy, Jr. Foundation, 14 October 1966.

———. "Practice Patterns of Women and Men Physicians." *Journal of Medical Education* 44 (June 1969): 481-91.

Pryor, June. "Women at Harvard Medical School." *Harvard Medical Alumni Bulletin* 29 (April 1954): 23-26.

"Report of the Professional Women of Stanford Medical School." Mimeographed. Stanford: Stanford University School of Medicine, December 1969.

Reuben, R. J. "Women in Medicine: Past, Present and Future." *Journal of the American Medical Women's Association* 27 (1972): 251-59.

Roback, G. A. *Distribution of Physicians in the U.S., 1973. Regional, State, County and Metropolitan Areas.* Chicago: American Medical Association, 1974.

Roeske, Nancy. "Women in Psychiatry: A Review." *American Journal of Psychiatry* 133 (1976): 365-72.

———. "Women in Medicine — A New Epoch." In preparation.

Roessler, R.; Collins, B.; and Mefford, R. B. "Sex Similarities in Medical School Applicants." *Journal of the American Medical Women's Association* 30 (1975): 254-65.

Romano, John. "More Point than Counterpoint." In *To Each His Farthest Star.* Rochester: University of Rochester Medical Center,

1975: 407–14.

Roper Organization, Inc. *The Virginia Slims American Women's Opinion Poll.* Vol. III. N.p., 1974.

Roselund, Mary Loretta, and Oski, Frank A. "Women in Medicine." *Annals of Internal Medicine* 66 (May 1967): 1008–12.

Rosen, R. A. Hudson. "Occupational Role Innovators and Sex Role Attitudes." *Journal of Medical Education* 49 (June 1974): 554–61.

Rossi, Alice S. "Barriers to the Career Choice of Engineering, Medicine, or Science Among American Women." In *Women and the Scientific Professions,* edited by Jacquelyn A. Mattfeld and Carol G. Van Aken. Cambridge: Massachusetts Institute of Technology Press, 1965: 51–127.

Rothstein, William G. *American Physicians in the Nineteenth Century: From Sects to Science.* Baltimore: John Hopkins Press, 1972.

Ruhe, C. H. "Memorandum to All Institutions with Accredited Programs in Medical Education." American Medical Association, 17 May 1976.

Ruthven, Helen. "Attachment of Local Authority Nurses to General Practice Prior to Reorganisation." *Health Bulletin* 34, no. 1 (1976): 29–35.

Shapiro, Carol S.; Stibler, Barbara-Jean; Zelkovic, Audrey A.; and Mausner, Judith. "Careers of Women Physicians: A Survey of Women Graduates from Seven Medical Schools, 1945–51. *Journal of Medical Education* 43 (October 1968): 1033–40.

Shapiro, Edith T. "Women Who Want to Be Women." *Woman Physician* 26 (1971): 399–413.

Shea, Petrena Abbe, and Pincock, Carolyn S. "A Census of Women Physicians in the Washington, D.C., Metropolitan Area." *Journal of the American Medical Women's Association* 21 (1966): 503–05.

Short, E. M. "Women in the AFCR: Present Status and Future Prospects." *Clinical Research* 24 (1976): 123.

Shryock, Richard H. "Women in American Medicine." *Journal of the American Medical Women's Association* 25 (1970): 371–79.

"Special Report of the Medical Education and Research Committee of the American Medical Women's Association." *Journal of the American Medical Women's Association* 27 (1972): 27.

Spitzer, W. O.; Hackett, B. C.; and Goldsmith, C. "Career Choices of Physicians 15 Years After Entering Medical School." *Canadian Medical Association Journal* 12 (22 February 1975).

Stephenson, Bette. *The President Speaks!* Saskatchewan: University of Saskatchewan, December 1974.

Steppacher, Robert C., and Mausner, Judith S. "Suicide in Male and

Female Physicians." *Journal of the American Medical Association,* 228, no. 3 (15 April 1974): 323–28.

Sullivan, Margaret P. "A New Era: Challenges for the Woman Physician." *Journal of the American Medical Women's Association* 29 (1974): 9–11.

Theodore, C. N.; Haug, J. N.; and Martin, B. C. *Special Statistical Series — Selected Characteristics of the Physician Population, 1963 and 1967.* Chicago: American Medical Association, 1968.

Tracy, Martha. "Women Graduates in Medicine." *Association of American Medical Colleges Bulletin* 2 (January 1927): 21–28.

Truax, R. *The Doctors Jacobi.* Boston: Little, Brown & Co., 1952.

Ulyatt, Kenneth, and Ulyatt, Frances M. "Some Attitudes of a Group of Women Doctors Related to Their Field Performance." *British Journal of Medical Education* 5 (1971): 242–45.

———. "Attitudes of Women Medical Students Compared with Those of Women Doctors." *British Journal of Medical Education* 7 (1973): 152–54.

U.S. Department of Commerce, Bureau of the Census. *The Labor Force.* United States Summary, Sixteenth Census of the United States, vol. 3, pt. 1. Washington: U.S. Government Printing Office, 1940.

———. *Characteristics of the Population.* United States Summary, Sixteenth Census of the United States, vol. 3, pt. 1, Washington: U.S. Government Printing Office, 1940.

———. Comparative Occupational Statistics for the United States, 1870–1940. Washington: U.S. Government Printing Office, 1943.

———. *1970 Occupation by Industry.* 1970 Census of Population, Special Report PC(2)-7C. Washington: Department of Commerce, 1972.

U.S. Department of Labor, Bureau of Labor Statistics. *Employment and Earnings* 21, no. 9. Washington: U. S. Department of Labor, n.d.: 91.

Verbrugge, Martha H. "Women and Medicine in Nineteenth-Century America." *Signs,* 1, no. 4 (Summer 1976): 957–72.

Vetter, Betty M., and Babco, Eleanor L. *Professional Women and Minorities.* Washington: Scientific Manpower Commission, February 1976.

Vincent, M. O.; Hill, M.; and Tathan, M. R. "Survey on Women Physicians." *Ontario Medical Review* 43, no. 7 (July 1976).

Waite, Frederick C. *History of the New England Female Medical College 1848–1874.* Boston: Boston University School of Medicine, 1950.

Walsh, Mary Roth. "Coping Mechanisms in Women Physicians." Interviews conducted in 1975 and 1976. Cambridge, Massachusetts: Radcliffe Institute.

Weinberg, Ethel, and Rooney, James F. "Academic Performance of Women Medical Students in Medical School." *Journal of Medical Education* 48 (March 1973): 240–47.

Westling-Wikstrand, Helena; Monk, Mary A.; and Thomas, Carolina B. "Some Characteristics Related to the Career Status of Women Physicians." *Johns Hopkins Medical Journal* 127 (1970): 273–86.

Williams, Phoebe A. "Women in Medicine: Some Themes and Variations." *Journal of Medical Education* 46 (July 1971): 584–91.

————. "Macy Fellowships for Women in Medicine: A Four-Year Experimental Program." Manuscript. June 1973.

Williams, Phoebe A., and Gamble, Frances P. "Radcliffe Medical Women." Paper prepared for Macy Conference on the Future of Women in Medicine, December 1968.

Witte, M. H.; Arem, A. J.; and Holguin, M. "Women Physicians in United States Medical Schools; Preliminary Report." *Journal of the American Medical Women's Association* 31 (1976): 211.

Women's Action Alliance. "Report to the Task Force in Health and Physical Safety, on Objective 8: Improve the Representation and Status of Women as Providers of Health Care Services and Increase the Responsibilities of Women in Health and Medical Care, National Women's Agenda." Mimeographed. New York: Women's Action Alliance, n.d.

Woodside, Nina. *Women in Medicine: Action Planning for the 1970's.* Resource booklet. Philadelphia: Center for Women in Medicine, 1974.

Wright, Katherine W. "History of Women in Medicine; A Symposium: Nineteenth Century or Transitional Period." *Bulletin of the Medical Library Association* 44 (January 1956): 16–22.

Yokopenic, Patricia A.; Bourque, Linda Brookover; and Brogan, Donna. "Professional Communication Networks: A Case Study of Women in the American Public Health Association." In *Social Problems.* N.p.: Society for the Study of Social Problems, 1975: 493–509.

Ziem, Grace. "Women and Health." *International Journal of Health Services* 5, no. 2 (1975): 167–71.

Participants

Margaret S. Bearn, LL.B.
Associate Dean
New York Law School
New York, New York

Mary I. Bunting, Ph.D.
President Emeritus
Radcliffe College

Alice S. Cary, M.D.
IBC Medical Supervisor's Office
Amherst House
Doshiba Women's College
Kyoto, Japan

Shirley G. Driscoll, M.D.
Professor of Pathology
Boston Hospital for Women
Chairperson: Joint Committee on
the Status of Women
Harvard Medical School
Boston, Massachusetts

Jack R. Ewalt, M.D.
Director
Mental Health and Behavioral Sciences
Department of Medicine and Surgery
Veterans Administration
Washington, D.C.

Lloyd C. Elam, M.D.
President
Meharry Medical College
Nashville, Tennessee

Patricia Albjerg Graham, Ph.D.
Dean
Radcliffe Institute
Cambridge, Massachusetts

Mary Ellen Hartman, M.D.
Associate Dean for Student Affairs
The Medical College of Pennsylvania
Philadelphia, Pennsylvania

Marilyn Heins, M.D.
Associate Dean for Student Affairs
School of Medicine
Wayne State University
Detroit, Michigan

Marion Jacobs, Ph.D.
Assistant Professor of Psychiatry
Lecturer in Social Ecology
Center for Counseling and Special
Services
School of Medicine
University of California, Irvine
Irvine, California

Joseph Katz, Ph.D.
Professor of Human Development
Director of Research for Human Development and Education Policy
State University of New York at
Stony Brook
Stony Brook, New York

Marion Kilson, Ph.D.
Director of Research
Radcliffe Institute
Cambridge, Massachusetts

Donald W. King, M.D.
Delafield Professor and Chairman
College of Physicians and Surgeons
Columbia University
New York, New York

117

Ms. Beatrice Levine
Project Director
Exploratory Study of Women in the
  Health Professions
Partner
Urban and Rural Systems Associations
San Francisco, California

Edithe J. Levit, M.D.
Vice President
National Board of Medical Examiners
Philadelphia, Pennsylvania

Leah M. Lowenstein, M.D., D.Phil.
*Associate Professor of Medicine and
  Assistant Dean*
School of Medicine
Boston University
Boston, Massachusetts

Una Maclean, M.D.
Senior Lecturer
Department of Community Medicine
Faculty of Medicine
University of Edinburgh
Edinburgh, Scotland

Elizabeth McAnarney, M.D.
*Assistant Professor of Pediatrics,
  Psychiatry, and Medicine*
Director of the Adolescent Program
School of Medicine and Dentistry
  and Strong Memorial Hospital
University of Rochester
Rochester, New York

Thomas H. Meikle, Jr., M.D.
Associate Dean
Office of Academic Programs
Cornell University Medical College
New York, New York

Vivian W. Pinn, M.D.
Assistant Dean for Student Affairs
School of Medicine
Tufts University
Boston, Massachusetts

Elva O. Poznanski, M.D.
Associate Professor of Psychiatry
The University of Michigan Medical
  School
Children's Psychiatric Hospital
Ann Arbor, Michigan

Theodore T. Puck, M.D.
Professor of Biophysics and Genetics
Director
Eleanor Roosevelt Institute for Cancer Research
University of Colorado Medical
  Center
Denver, Colorado

Nancy A. Roeske, M.D.
Professor of Psychiatry
Director
Undergraduate Curriculum, Department of Psychiatry
School of Medicine
Indiana University
Indianapolis, Indiana

Ricky Schachter, M.D.
Associate Professor
Department of Medicine
Faculty of Medicine
University of Toronto
Women's College Hospital
Toronto, Ontario, Canada

Marjorie S. Sirridge, M.D.
Senior Docent and Professor
School of Medicine
University of Missouri, Kansas City
Kansas City, Missouri

Jan Soulé, M.D.
Fellow in Ambulatory Pediatrics
Primary Care Center
School of Medicine
University Hospital
University of California, San Diego
San Diego, California

J. Robert Willson, M.D.
Professor and Chairman
Department of Obstetrics and Gynecology
The University of Michigan Medical School
Ann Arbor, Michigan

Marjorie P. Wilson, M.D.
Director
Department of Institutional Development
Association of American Medical Colleges
Washington, D. C.

Program

§

(Anyone wishing to obtain copies of the papers
listed should write to the individual authors.)

Tuesday, September 7   Historical Review of Women in Medicine in
the United States
Marion Kilson

Wednesday, September 8   Report of a Study of the Impact of Women in
United States Medical Schools
Elizabeth McAnarney

College Women's Career Aspirations—
Changing Attitudes for Medicine
Joseph Katz

Selecting Women for Medical School
Thomas H. Meikle, Jr.

Women Medical Students: Their Characteristics and Concerns
Marion Jacobs

Special Career Considerations: Advising
Women Medical Students
Vivian W. Pinn

Women in Residency Training: Changing Patterns
Leah M. Lowenstein

Discussant: Jan Soulé

Thursday, September 9   Women in Medicine in Scotland
Una Maclean

Career Patterns of Women in Medicine
Marjorie P. Wilson

Discussant: Marilyn Heins

121

Opportunities for Women in Legal Careers
Margaret S. Bearn

Opportunities for Women in Academic Medicine
Elva O. Poznanski

Friday, September 10

Opportunities for Women in Medical Careers in Canada: Before and After Provincial Health Services
Ricky Schachter

Women in Medicine in Japan
Alice S. Cary

Strategy for Research Programs Relating to Women in Medical Education and Medical Careers in the United States
Mary I. Bunting

Index

🌿

AAMC. *See* Association of American Medical Colleges

Academic advisors, 24–25

Academic medical centers. *See* Medical schools

Administration, 35
See also Leadership roles

Admissions, 15–21
and age discrimination, 20–21
committees, 19–20, 54
historical perspective, 1–2
interviews, 17–19
Medical College Admission Test, 15–16
problems, 4–5
recent trends, 2–4
recommendations for action, 5–7
statistical data, 15, 16, 18, 19

Advisory services. *See* Supportive services

Affirmative action, 25, 33, 35, 38

Age discrimination, and admissions policies, 20–21

American Medical Women's Association, 42

American Public Health Association, 98

Association of American Medical Colleges (AAMC), 97
executive development program, 99
report on medical school faculties, 33–34

Astin, H. S., 33, 36

Attitudes
of older female faculty, 30, 39, 56

toward female medical students, 3, 18–19, 29–30, 54
toward women physicians, 12, 100–01
See also Discrimination

Attrition rates, 16

Bayer, A. E., 33, 36

Blackwell, Elizabeth, 9

Bunting, Mary I., 1–7, 80

Career conflicts, 82–83
See also Family; Marriage

Career patterns, 40–41, 84–85, 89–104
employment characteristics, 93–95
health care careers, 86–87, 90–91
leadership roles, 97–99, 102
marriage and family, 39–41, 95, 99–100
salaries, 92–95
specialties, 91–92, 93
See also specific main headings,
e.g. Health care careers; Leadership roles

Cary, Alice S., 82, 83

Child care, 4, 42–43
problems, 50, 82

Civil Rights Act of 1964, Title VII, 33

Committees on the status of women
Joint Committee on the Status and Tenure of Women, 20
Professional Women at Stanford Medical School, 20

123